SHEFFIELD'S EVIL WOMEN

Margaret Drinkall

Chris Drinkall

Contents

Introduction

Women who transgressed the law in 19th century Sheffield were seen as deviant, evil and out of control, and they were an anathema to the more 'respectable' people of the town. In most cases, they were not objectively "evil", they turned to crime, because they had to, in order to survive. Whether that crime was prostitution or stealing articles from shops to pawn, it might be the only way of feeding themselves or their families. In a world where the tremors of feminism had barely begun, these women were marked as "evil" and they deserved punishment.

Many were punished by being transported to a foreign country, thousands of miles distant from Sheffield. Their crimes may have been stealing a few shillings, or stealing some boots and some brushes. One appalling woman threw her daughter into the Rivelin Dam, to tragic cases of women killing their own newborn babies, in order to hide their crime, of unmarried conception.

Some committed crimes against other women. Such as using the art of fortune telling, to relieve someone of their money, or even causing a young girl, who thought she was doomed, to kill herself. There was an ignorant midwife, whose succeeded in killing two women with her incompetence. But perhaps the woman most feared by the Sheffield authorities were the prostitutes. They were seen as corrupting innocent young men out of their well-earned wages. Sheffield in the 19th century was seen as a hotbed of vice, and the women who worked in such professions as the most depraved imaginable

All these cases are true and really happened in Sheffield during the nineteenth century. As our modern world still struggles with the vestiges of inequality, it is fascinating to cast our gaze back across a century of social upheaval, to a time, as abhorrent to us now, as medieval times must have surely seemed to Victorian society.

Margaret and Chris Drinkall
March 2021

Chapter One: Transported Sheffield Women.

In the eyes of society, the most evil kind of women were those who committed crimes, yet most of those crimes were simply common theft. By the beginning of the nineteenth century, women who had committed thefts on more than one occasion, could now be transported to Australia for a term of either 7 – 14 years. The majority of these women now faced situations they had never ever dreamt about before. Many of them had never been in a rowing boat before, were now facing a six months sea journey in a convict ship, followed by years of exile.

One such Sheffield woman who was transported to Australia following her conviction was a woman called Jane Brickhill. In October 1825 Jane was charged with stealing 12s in silver from the person of a young man called John Mooney on the night of 15 October. By this time Jane, who was also known to be a prostitute, had following a long criminal career and was seen as a hardened criminal. Mooney on the other hand was described as 'a youth under the age of 20 years' who told the court that the prisoner had made an appointment to meet him, at 11 pm, in the Hartshead, Sheffield.

When he met her, the youth had put his arm around her in an affectionate manner, but instead of it being reciprocated, Jane had thrust her hand roughly into his breeches pocket and taken the sum of 12 shillings. A night watchman called Thomas Morton was the first witness and he told the bench that he had been patrolling in the area, when he heard shouting. He ran to the sound and came upon the pair who he found scuffling together on the ground. The young man told him that Jane had stolen some money from him, and Morton took her into custody.

Mooney also accompanied the prisoner and escort back to the station in order to make his statement, and on the way Jane told him she would give him back his money if he refused to give evidence against her. She also offered the night watchman 2s to let her go, but they both ignored her. Jane was very well aware that with her criminal history, there was a good chance that she would now face transportation instead of a custodial sentence. When they reached the police station she was searched and the sum of 13s 6d was found on different parts of her person.

At the magistrates court three days later, the prisoner was allowed to ask questions and she challenged Mooney that he had been with several girls in the Hartshead that night, and it was one of those who had robbed him. Showing her desperation, Jane then claimed that rather than making an appointment to meet him, she had been on her way home when he had stopped her. The prisoner said that he then accused her of stealing his money without any provocation. However her previous history was against her, so it must have come as no shock when the jury took just an hour to return with a verdict of guilty.

The magistrate told the court that the prisoner had been before the Sheffield bench now on three or four different occasions. Turning to Jane he told her that 'her practice and example were of so pernicious a description that he could not ignore them'. The magistrate then ordered that the prisoner be transported for seven years. Jane showed absolutely no remorse as she cheekily told him 'Thank you Sir, had you done this eight years ago, you might have made a woman of me. As a result it was reported that on Saturday 22 October 1825 Jane Brickhill and two male prisoners who had also been sentenced to seven years transportation were put on the Ebor Coach at Sheffield on route for York Castle.

There they would be imprisoned until arrangements could be made for their transportation Records shows that on 8 December, Jane Brickhill was put on the convict ship 'Providence' along with another 99 female prisoners. The ship arrived at Van Diemans Land (later called Tasmania) on 16 May 1826, and it is unlikely that Jane ever saw Sheffield again.

Research of some of the diaries left behind by people like the convict ships surgeons, indicate that many of these female prisoners who suffered these early transportations, had never so much as experienced leaving their home town before. Consequently many of them fell victim to terrible sea sickness, as they lay on their beds in the lowest part of the vessel. No allowances were made for the fact that they were women, as they all had to endure the same harsh regime as the male convicts, both during the sea journey and after they had landed ashore. Many of these women would be placed in domestic service in this new land, whilst others would serve out their time in factories.

Another transported convict was a young Sheffield woman called Charlotte Phillips who was aged 20 when she was tried at the Pontefract Sessions on 3 April 1826 for stealing a cash box. It had belonged to a beer house keeper of Sheffield called William Ward. He was the first witness and he told the court that on 25 February 1826 the box contained a substantial amount of money. He claimed that inside there was a £30 Bank of England note, a £10 note, three £5 notes, seven £1 notes, some guineas and other cash amounting to £67.13s. Ward said that he knew that the money had been in his possession the day before, when the prisoner had been employed at his public house as a cleaner.

He stated that the box was hidden inside another box which was usually kept locked. He told the bench that on that day he had been doing some brewing, when Charlotte went to his wife and asked her for some dinner. The prisoner was given some food and he said that after finishing her shift, she went home around 4.30 pm. Shortly after that he missed both the box and his daughter Mary Ward aged nine. Enquiring in the town, he found that Charlotte and his daughter had taken a Waterloo carriage to Rotherham. He reported the theft to the Sheffield police and one of the watchmen of the town, a man called John Lindley made enquiries.

On 24 February Lindley found that Charlotte and the child were staying in Rotherham at the lodgings of a woman called 'Widow Guest.' Lindley went there armed with a warrant to arrest Charlotte Phillips and with instructions to bring back the daughter of William Ward. He claimed that he had identified the prisoner by holding his lantern close to her face as he told her to 'give me the money you stole at Sheffield'. The woman immediately put her hand into her pocket and handed over £55. 4s of the stolen money, admitting that she had spent the rest.

Lindley took Charlotte into custody where she confessed that she had persuaded the child, Mary to rob her father and had promised that she would take her to Rotherham and buy her things from the proceeds. The next day Charlotte Phillips was brought before the Sheffield magistrates, where she was found guilty and sent to take her trial at the next Pontefract Sessions. At the Sessions the child Mary Ward was the first witness and she gave evidence against Charlotte in front of magistrate and MP, Mr Stuart Wortley Esq., and Hugh Parker Esq.

It was reported that the girl was quite intelligent for her years and she spoke up quite well. Mary told the court that her father had been occupied brewing up some beer on 25 February 1826 when Charlotte Phillips asked her where her father kept his money. The girl told him that it was in a box, but that it was always kept locked inside another box. When the prisoner asked Mary if she could get the key, the girl agreed and shortly afterwards she gave the prisoner the key. The young witness said that Charlotte then opened the first box and took out the cash box and she went away with it.

The girl claimed that in order to divert suspicion, it had been agreed beforehand that she would meet Charlotte half an hour later in Sheffield town centre. Once she met up with Charlotte, the witness said that the prisoner had bought her a new bonnet and shawl before they both took the carriage to Rotherham. One of the magistrates asked Mary Ward had she actually given the box to the prisoner, which she denied.

John Lindley gave evidence of his arresting Charlotte Phillips, before the prisoner was asked if she had anything to say in her own defence. She had been listening carefully to all the evidence against her, and so she had plenty to say. She told the court that Mary Ward had lied and that it was she who had brought the cash box to her home and given it to her. It was at her urging that they agreed to travel to Rotherham together in order to escape detection. She referred to her employer William Ward as a liar and claimed that he was well know in Sheffield as 'Blue Billy.'

Charlotte told the court that she was not employed as a cleaner, but that she was a lodger at the beer house for which she paid 4s a week rent. The prisoner angrily told the court that 'Blue Billy' was notorious for letting out rooms at the beer house for a few hours to girls who had their living to earn. Charlotte stated that he was well known to be a 'bad man' and that he 'had sworn falsely against her'. Angrily she claimed that she had never been employed as a cleaner, and had never asked his wife for food.

The chair of the magistrates in passing sentence stated that the prisoner had aggravated her own crime by seducing a young innocent girl into criminal activity. He then ordered Charlotte Phillips to transportation for seven years and she was removed, protesting angrily all the way to the cells.

But if William Ward thought he had escaped punishment he was wrong. He was then informed by Mr Stuart Wortley that he had to once more take his place in the witness box. Reminding him that he was still under oath, the magistrate told him that his occupation and character was indeed 'well known to the legal authorities of Sheffield'.

He said that the money in the cash box was no doubt booty from his infamous trade of letting out rooms to the abandoned women of the town. He told him 'you have been a lucky man in obtaining your property again, but in the event of a second robbery I can assure you that no one would pity you'. Ward made the excuse that as the rent and taxes he had to pay were so high, that he had been necessitated to keep such a house as he had. However he assured Mr Wortley that he had since discharged all the girls in the rooms and meant not to trade in such a way again.

The chair said that he was glad to hear that and he hoped that Ward spoke the truth. He was then warned of his future behaviour, before being dismissed. On Saturday 26 August 1826, Charlotte Phillips was removed from York Castle where she had been kept since her trial, to be delivered aboard a hulk at Woolwich. These were old ships which had were permanently moored after being de-commissioned and where prisoners were kept awaiting transportation. This is where Charlotte awaited the next part of her journey. On 31 August the convict ship 'Sir Charles Forbes' set sail along with 70 other female convicts before the ship landed at Van Diemans Land on 3 January 1827.

Another transported Sheffield woman was called Catherine Whitham aged 28, who was also charged with stealing money, as well as a snuff box and other articles from the person of William Willoughby at Sheffield in July 1849. She had been charged with a man called Charles Hancock who was seen as the prime instigator in the crime. Consequently he was given 14 years transportation and she was ordered to be transported for seven years. She was placed on the convict ship the 'St Vincent' along with 205 other female prisoners. They left England on 13 December 1849 and arrived at Van Diemen's Land on 4 April 1850.

Sheffield magistrates when sentencing young women like Charlotte Phillips or Catherine Whitham might easily ease their conscience about the severity of the sentence, by assuming that such women would be welcome in their new country. It was thought that there was a shortage of women in Van Diemans Land and as most of the convicts were aged between 20 – 30 years, they would soon marry and settle down to an honest life. However that excuse did not work for older women, who they just as harshly condemned.

One such Sheffield women called Ann Lenton was brought before the magistrates on Friday 29 October 1841. The arresting officer told the court that despite her advanced age she had been convicted several times for the petty crime of larceny. He said that on this last occasion, Ann had been found guilty of stealing a pair of boots and several brushes belonging to a soldier who had been quartered at the Black Swan Inn. The magistrates after hearing all the evidence told her:

'It is a melancholy thing to see you, an old woman in such a position. It appears that your habit of plunder were so inveterate, that it is necessary to prevent you for continuing to indulge them.'

He then sentenced her to transportation for seven years.

Ann cried piteously as he said this and cried out 'Oh pray don't do that to an old woman.' But the man was unrepentant as he told her 'you have been here six times before!' Ann Lenton was sent aboard the convict ship the 'Royal Admiral' on 2 May 1842 along with 203 other women. They arrived in Van Diemen's Land on 24 September 1842 to begin their exile. It is to be hoped that Ann had a good life in Australia for the short time she had left to live.

These then are some of the Sheffield women who were transported out of Britain. Records show that many of them did manage to establish new lives for themselves, often marrying other convicts and having children whose forebears remain in Australia today. Many of these ancestors are now quite proud of their convicted forebears and happily describe them as 'Australian Royalty'. If those Sheffield women sent out of England for their crimes, could have looked into their own future, I wonder what they would have thought!

Chapter Two: Martha Bagshaw.

Throughout the nineteenth century the main 'crime' committed by women was that of single girls giving birth to illegitimate children. There was little legal recourse to law in those days for the mothers of these children, as the only way in which the man could be held responsible was if the woman took him before the magistrates on a bastardy charge. The bench would then order him to pay weekly maintenance for the child. However most men simply denied that they were the father, and unless the girl had some proof in the form of a letter, she would not be believed. So the only option was to try to deal with the birth in what ever way she could.

Some girls finding themselves in this terrifying situation, visited abortionists if they could afford it. Others simply denied that they were pregnant, blaming it on an illness like dropsy. But all of them faced the problem of what to do with the child when it was born. Consequently it is a tragic fact that the streets of Sheffield were filled with abandoned or dead babies. Only as the century wore on did the legal authorities begin to soften in their approach to such girls, which is demonstrated by the cases in this book.

In the beginning such women were charged with wilful murder which was a capital offence. Only later did they reduce it to concealment of birth, which resulted in a prison sentence. In 1839 a Sheffield woman called Martha Bagshaw who was 28 years old, was found to be the mother of such a child. She was living and working at a public house in Grimesthorpe, Sheffield called the Bowling Green Tavern, which was run by Mr John Marshall and his wife. Martha knew very well that if she admitted to being pregnant, she would lose her position and be unable to provide for herself.

Mrs Marshall had watched Martha putting on weight and she suspected that she was pregnant, but Martha continued to deny it. Matters were brought to a head however on Tuesday 17 September 1839 when the Marshall's grand daughter Agnes aged 12 came to visit. She was sent to sleep in the same bed as the servant. The young girl complained later the next day that she had been greatly disturbed by Martha who had been very restless in bed that night. At one point Agnes thought she heard a child cry, but Martha told her it was just the wind whistling in the trees outside.

However, as the light of morning came into the bedroom, Martha admitted that she wasn't feeling too good and Agnes wanted to call her grandmother, but the girl told her not to as she would feel much better soon. The child fell asleep again and a few hours later Martha arose to start work. As she was dressing, she told Agnes not to tell her grandparents about her not being very well the night before, and Agnes agreed that she wouldnt. However Mrs Marshall's keen eyes had noticed the sudden change in her servants body shape and she accused her of having given birth to a child during the night.

Martha denied it at first, but Mrs Marshall persisted in her accusations, until finally the girl broke down and confessed. She claimed that she had given birth, but the child had been still born and she had buried it in the manure heap in the fold yard at the back of the Bowling Green Tavern. Mrs Marshall told her that she would have to report the matter to the police authorities and she sent for a constable. Sometime later an officer arrived at the house and Martha pointed out to the place in the fold yard where she had buried the body.

The constable borrowed a spade and started digging and about six inches down he came upon the little body wrapped in rags. It could see that it was a full grown female child and it lay upon its back. Going back into the kitchen, he asked Martha who the father of the child was, and she told him it was William Coates, a file cutter of New Edward Street, Sheffield. The constable then went to Martha parents house and interviewed them as to whether they knew anything about their daughter being pregnant. Martha's father said that he loved his daughter, but that sometimes she was 'just not right in her mind' due to an abject betrayal by the man she had loved.

Mr Bagshaw explained that Coates had promised to marry Martha and he had persuaded her to leave the domestic service position where she had previously worked, and to come back to Sheffield in order to prepare for their wedding. Martha was excited as she and a friend scoured the town looking for a house where she and Coates would live after the wedding. Only later did it transpire that her intended husband had married her unnamed friend instead. The constable made a note to this effect and then he reported to the Chief Constable of Sheffield.

The Coroner Mr T Badger Esq., was also informed of the death and he arranged for an inquest to be held at the Bowling Green Tavern on Monday 23 September 1839. The first witness was Martha's father who described to the court his daughter's betrayal by her lover. He was followed on the stand by Martha's mother, Mrs Bagshaw and she too spoke of her daughter as 'not being quite right in the head'. Mr Badger asked her how this manifested itself, but she vaguely answered that 'she had sometimes thought that Martha was not so sharp as she would like her to be'.

The foreman of the jury asked for more clarification, but the coroner interrupted and told the jury that they were not there to assess the prisoner's state of mind, but to enquire how the child came to its death. At this point Mr Badger stated that he intended adjourning the enquiry to the following day in the hope that the prisoner would be fully recovered enough to be able to attend the inquest for herself in order to give her own evidence. He had also asked for a post mortem to be completed. He told the inquest that the enquiry and the surgeons report would be heard at the Coroners Office the following afternoon.

The first witness at the re-convened inquest was surgeon Mr William Jackson who gave evidence that he had examined the body of the child earlier that morning. He said that the indications were that the child had been born a few days previously and it had been full term. Mr Jackson gave the length of the child which was 19 ½ inches and the fact that it weighed 5lbs 6½ ozs at birth. He said that externally there had been some injuries on the body, which had including an indentation on the right cheek. When asked by the coroners what might have caused such an injury he said it was as if it had been pressed with a finger or some hard substance.

The child's eyes were black, and bruising was visible over the ribs and the right side of the chest area. One way in which the medical evidence would prove that the child had led a separate existence from its mother (or in other words that it had been born alive) was the state of the lungs.

Mr Jackson said that the lungs were perfectly healthy and they had floated when placed in water, indicating that the child had taken a breath after it had been born. The surgeon concluded that from his examination of the child's body that he had no doubt that the child had been born alive.

The room was then cleared and the jury began their deliberations together. It took about an hour before they returned back into the inquest room and gave a verdict that Martha Bagshaw had committed the wilful murder of her newly born child. The coroner issued his warrant for the committal of the prisoner to York to take her trial at the next assizes. Martha Bagshaw appeared at the York Spring Assizes on Thursday 12 March 1840 in front of judge, Mr Justice Erskine charged with the murder of her child.

This must have been a truly terrifying ordeal for any woman charged with such a crime, confronted with the all male officers of the court, along with all its attendant pomp and artificiality. The judge would be sitting in his magisterial chair adorned in his red robes, and the prosecution and defence counsels wearing their wigs must have been a most daunting sight. Needless to say, it was reported that Martha looked terrified as she stood in the dock. As was usual in those days, the prisoner was undefended.

In a trembling voice the prisoner pleaded not guilty to the charge of wilful murder, however she pleaded guilty to the lesser crime of concealment of birth. Mr Heaton was the prosecution and he outlined the case for the jury, where thankfully he too advocated a conviction on the lesser charge of concealment for the prisoner. Martha Bagshaw received what was described as an 'excellent admonition' from the judge, before he sentenced her to prison for 12 months with hard labour. Martha was lucky as a few years earlier the same crime would have been described as infanticide for which she would have faced the death penalty and would have been hanged as a result.

To my mind girls like Martha (of which there is a few more in this book) could not be thought of as 'evil' in any way. They were simply victims of lust for which the putative father got away scot-free. Nevertheless I have included them in this book of evil woman as that's how they would have been seen by society and the legal authorities of the period. Women in such situations were seen by the more 'respectable' members of society as having brought the problem on themselves, simply by giving way to their own passions. By giving birth to an illegitimate child and having to care for it was ample punishment for that so-called crime.

Chapter Three: Ann Law.

Sadly not all child murders were those of a newly born infant. Less clear was why mothers would attempt to murder an older child, especially when the child was six years of age. Researching this case, it seems obviously that this woman's mind was a most disturbed one. The loss of her husband and being left with the responsibility for a child, had perhaps unhinged her reason. Mental health problems were less understood in the nineteenth century, and there was no treatment available for them. Brought before the legal authorities, no such allowances were made for the condition of their minds.

On Saturday 4 January 1840 a woman and her six year old child were seen walking around the Rivelin Mill dam. This was a local beauty spot visited by many people of Sheffield during the summer at weekends, to get away from the grime and unsanitary conditions in the town itself. However what happened next was totally unexpected. Looking around to make sure no one was watching, the woman slipped one of her garters off her leg and put it tightly around the little child's throat in one swift movement. Then, picking up the little girl up she threw her into the water.

Without a backward glance the woman then hastened away as the child struggled in the water. Thankfully the girl was able to make her way to the bank and pull herself out of the waters icy depths. She lay on the bank panting until a man, a carter called Jonathan Hill came along. He saw the exhausted state of the girl and took her to the nearby Surrey Arms public house at Hollow Meadows, where she was cared for by Mrs Sarah Greaves the landlords wife. The police were notified and Constable Deakin soon arrived and asked the girl her name.

She told him it was Mary Ann Law and it had been her mother Ann Law who had thrown her into the Rivelin dam. She described her mother to the constable and the woman was later found two miles away on the road to Sheffield. Ann Law was arrested and taken into custody, where she told the police that she was a widow, who lived in lodgings on Meadow Street, Sheffield and had come to the town from Barnsley a few months previously. Two days later the woman was brought before the magistrates charged with the attempted murder of her daughter. At the time she was described as being 'a young woman, decently dressed in black'.

After hearing some preliminary evidence, the prisoner was remanded until the following Friday 10 January 1840. The first witness at the next court appearance was Sarah Greaves who told the bench that she was the landlady of the Surrey Arms public house. She said the child had been brought to her house by Jonathan Hill on 4 January and the witness described how the girl was dripping wet and looking very bedraggled. Mrs Greaves told the magistrates how she had undressed the little girl to dry her, and that's when she had found the garter wrapped tightly around the girls neck. As she removed it, there was a red mark where the garter had been.

The landlady said the child remained at the Surrey Arms until the following day when Constable Crapper took her and the garter away. Once again the prisoner was remanded until Friday 24 January. By the time Ann next appeared, she was already being described as 'an unnatural mother' by the local press. The prosecution was Mr Marples who said that the first witness he was going to call was that of the child herself. One of the magistrates, Mr Chandler questioned the competence of such a young witness, but Mr Marples assured him that she was a very intelligent girl.

Mary Ann then told the court an horrendous story of the way in which her mother had tried to kill her. She said that her father had been James Law, and they had previously lived in Barnsley until his death. The girl said that after his death, herself and her mother had taken lodgings on Meadow Street, Sheffield with a woman called Mrs Otley. Mary Ann then described the day of the incident. She told how she and her mother had gone to visit her aunt Bessy who lived at Crookes, where they stayed until dinner time. The girl described the long walk they had then taken alongside the Dam until she complained to her mother that she was tired.

Her mother seem to be not listening and then suddenly they stopped and she and her mother threw stones in the water for a while as the girl rested. Mary Ann said that suddenly and without warning, her mother picked her up and threw her in the water. The water came over her head and the girl described how she struggled until she managed to get to the bank of a field and pulled herself out of the dam. She told a hushed courtroom that at that point her mother came up to her again and this time took off one of her garters which she put around Mary Ann's neck.

She said it was so tight that she could not cry or speak. Then, once more she picked the girl up and threw her again in the water. The young witness described how her mother then cruelly thrown stones at her and one of them hit her on the hand before her mother turned and walked away. Once again this brave child managed to pull herself out of the water. She had been in the water for some time and by now was completely exhausted when she reached the safety of the bank. The child then described how, as she lay there panting until a man came up and he spoke kindly to her. When she told him what had happened, he lifted her into the cart he had been driving.

The carter Jonathon Hill was the next witness and he described how he was going home about 2 pm on that Saturday after some business had taken him to Sheffield. About four miles out of the town on the Glossop Road, he saw a woman, who he now identified as the prisoner, coming towards him. The witness described how he passed her and then noticed that she looked upset and concerned. He turned round to look at her at the same time as she turned around to look at him. Hill said that there was something about the woman which disturbed him. When he got half a mile further, near to the Rivelin dam the witness saw a little girl on the ground moaning and gasping.

As he went up to her she held her hands up to him. He could see that she was wet through and he jumped down off the cart and ran to the girls side. She told him she wanted to go home and as he put her in his cart, he asked where her mother was. The girl told him she had left her and Hill remembered the woman he had passed earlier. When he arrived at the Rivelin Windmill, the witness said he stopped the cart and asked the miller Joseph Grey to try to stop the woman he had just passed on Glossop Road. Hill described her and then told the miller that she had tried to murder her child as he indicating the little girl in the cart. Joseph Grey immediately got into his own cart and went after the woman.

Meanwhile the witness said he took the child to the Surrey Arms. There the child was cared for by Mrs Greaves, and he too saw the garter which the landlady had taken off the girls neck. The next witness was the miller Joseph Grey. He said that before the last witness arrived at the mill he was crossing the road with his sheep. Earlier he had seen the prisoner and her daughter going down towards the dam and the child had looked happy and playful as she skipped along holding onto her mothers hand. When Hill had told him what had happened, he set off in pursuit of the woman and overtook her on the road. Grey informed her that her daughter had managed to get out of the water, and that he knew that she had throw her in.

He told the prisoner 'what a wretched woman you must needs be'. The prisoner then asked Grey if she could take the child and go, but he told her she must go back with him and the witness said he took her to his mill. On the way back Grey asked her how she could have done such a thing, but Ann Law simply told him that she could not keep the child. Once he got back to his mill, he sent one of his men to find a constable and a short time later Constable Crapper arrived. Hill told him what had happened, before handing the woman over to the officer. The constable then appeared as the next witness.

Police Constable Crapper showed the garter to the courtroom and he described taking the prisoner into custody. The bench then discussed the case before find Ann Law guilty of the attempted murder of her daughter Mary Ann. They sent her to take her trial at the next assizes. Ann Law appeared before the York Assizes on Saturday 21 March 1840 where she pleaded guilty. Mr Baines for the prosecution outlined the case for the jury. He described the attempt to drown the child, although he admitted that previously the prisoner had behaved very well towards the child.

Therefore he suggested that the prisoner had committed the act whilst 'labouring under an aberration of the mind'. The judge took no notice of this however as he sentenced Ann Law to be imprisoned at Wakefield House of Correction for 18 months with hard labour.

This case is a puzzle mainly because the voice of the perpetrator was not heard in the newspaper recordings of the time. No doubt if the poor woman was labouring under some kind of mental illness, she would not be able to properly defend herself in a court of law. As was usual at the time, Ann Law had no defence counsel to speak for her and was undoubtedly unable to give her own side of the matter. To have kept a child for six years and then when her husband died and left her without any income, Ann would be forced to either go into the workhouse or live a life of destitution. To have subjected her daughter to that kind of life must have affected the way she thought.

It is to be hoped that being in prison, and under the care of the surgeon who would notice such thing, such mental health issues would finally have been noted. Although there were no medication or treatment for such issues, it is to be hoped that she might have some more specialist care. As for her daughter Mary Ann, she would have to grow up without her mother and little understanding of why her mother tried to kill her that day at the Rivelin dam.

Chapter Four: Sarah Kay.

In 1840 the great improvements in the postal system of Great Britain was set in place by the introduction of the Penny Post. Now anyone from any class, could send letters weighing no more than ½ oz to anywhere in the country. As a result of this, postal deliveries were improved and co-ordinated by the institution of Post Offices. These were set up to receive, register and send onto their destination any letters that that were handed in and postage paid. As some of these letters contained cash, naturally the post office employees were vetted carefully, as they were in a position of great responsibility. Inevitably, some fell by the wayside and one of those was a woman in charge of the Glossop Road post office.

In June 1844 Sarah Kay who was aged 37 years was described as the 'keeper' of the post office. She was said to be diligent and keen, but nevertheless some letters had gone missing and she was suspected of committing four acts of felony. Consequently she was brought before the Sheffield magistrates on Thursday 27 June 1844. The case had been instigated by a man known as the Superintendent of the Missing Letter Department of the General Post Office. His name was Mr John Ramsey and right at the opening of the case he left Sarah in no doubt as what punishment she could expect if found guilty. He told the court that the Post Office rules stated that:

'Every person employed under the Post Office who shall steal, embezzle, secrete or destroy a post letter, shall either be transported for seven years, or be imprisoned for a term not exceeding three years. If any such letter shall contain any chattel, money or valuable security, they shall be transported for life'.

Mr Ramsey proceeded to charge Sarah with stealing four letters from the Glossop Road branch, which he then listed. The first, which was addressed to Mrs Moore, care of Mrs Hicks, of Chancery Lane, London, had been reported missing and the letter had contained two half sovereigns. Another missive addressed to Mrs Mason, 4 Brunswick Place, Brompton, London had also gone missing. As had a third letter addressed to Miss Spencer, of Nobut near Uttoxeter and a fourth to Mr R Parker, Bannister Court, Small Street, Liverpool.

However Mr Ramsey admitted that up to that point, he had only prepared evidence for two of the letters. The prosecutor stated that he had been asked to look into the loss of several letters, which had been directed through the Glossop Road post office and which he suspected had been stolen by the prisoner. He said that in order to investigate the matter, he had arrived in Sheffield on 24 June 1844 intending to make some preliminary enquiries. The next day, as a test he had deposited several letters containing silver coins into the receiving box at Glossop Road. Later in the day they were sent to the Sheffield main office, where he noted that two of the letters had already been opened.

On the same day Mr Ramsey deposited a letter in which he placed two marked half sovereigns which were fixed in a piece of card and sealed with black wax. Written on the envelope were the words 'handle with care' and 'paid'. Only one of the half sovereigns and the card had been delivered, and he held up the remaining card to show it to the court. He pointed out that the seal was not the same as he had put on, and it was very obvious that the seal had clearly been cut through.

Mr Ramsey said that on Wednesday morning 26 June 1844 he reported the thefts to the Superintendent of Police at Sheffield, Mr Raynor who got a warrant to search Sarah Kay's house and post office. Accompanied by the Superintendent, the two men went to undertake the search. As they told Sarah Kay what they intended to do, Mr Raynor saw the prisoner surreptitiously drop a leather bag behind the counter. When he picked it up and searched it, there was the card and the marked half sovereign inside, which was identified by himself.

Also in the bag were three half crowns and 2s 3d in silver and copper, and a small packet of coffee. He showed these items to Mr Ramsey who identified them before the superintendent caught hold of Sarah and placed her in handcuffs. Then Mr Raynor addressed the court and described how on Wednesday morning at 10.30 am, the two men had knocked on the door of the post office and it had been opened by the prisoner. An assistant to Sarah Kay was also in the room and she told the two men that her name was Phoebe Ogden.

The superintendent explained who Mr Ramsey was and why they had gone there, due to the fact that several letters had gone missing. Mr Raynor urged the guilty person to make a full confession. He also glanced at Phoebe Ogden, but Sarah immediately stepped forward and told him 'Do not blame her, I alone am guilty and I must bear the penalty'. Mr Raynor then described examining the leather bag and arresting the prisoner before he went to the upstairs rooms of the post office. There he found several letters in a wire basket and among them was the one direct to Mrs Moore.

Returning back to the kitchen he began to search it when the prisoner tried to forestall him. Taking out a newspaper from a drawer, Sarah opened it up and placed inside it was a letter from Mrs Mason which had been opened. Inside the letter was a silk handkerchief, which Mr Raynor also showed to the court. In a drawer in the front room were the missing letters directed to Robert Parker and Miss Spencer. He also found a small seal which held the same as the impression in the wax on the letter to Mrs Moore. The prisoner was then arrested on the charge of felony.

Miss M A Ellison of St Phillips Road Sheffield was the next witness and she told the bench that on 21 June she wrote a letter to a Mrs Mason of 4 Brunswick Place, Brompton, London. Enclosed inside it was a small silk handkerchief. Miss Ellison said that she took the package herself to the post office on Glossop Road and handed it to the prisoner. Sarah had told her that the postage for the package would cost 2d which the witness handed over to her. The witness said that in mitigation she had taken letters to the same post office which had all been delivered safely.

The next witness was a woman called Miss Jane Wreaks who also worked for the post office. She told the bench that under Mr Ramsden's instructions, she had prepared a letter and had given it to a friend to post with a penny to pay for the postage. She had instructed her to take the letter and make sure that she deposited it at the Glossop Road office. The friend Elizabeth Middleton confirmed the previous witnesses account and said that she had given the letter to the assistant who worked for Sarah Kay called Phoebe Ogden.

Miss Ogden told the magistrates that she had worked for Sarah Kay for three or four years and for some time past she had been instructed to take in the post when the post mistress was out. She stated that usually all letters to be directed were sent in a bag, which was tied up with string and sealed with wax at the close of the day. These were then sent to the main Sheffield Office to be directed on. Any letters or packages that came after that time, were forwarded in a wire basket. On that Tuesday she had received several letters and postages which she had put into a drawer.

Miss Ogden said that as Sarah Kay had then returned, so for the rest of her day she had been working up stairs at Glossop Road or on other duties. Mr Ramsden asked her if she remembered receiving a letter which had been sent by Miss Jane Wreaks, but she replied that she could not remember such a letter. The magistrates, after hearing all the evidence quickly found Sarah Kay guilty and she was sent to take her trial.

When Sarah appeared at the York Assizes on Monday 15 July 1844 she appeared to be deeply affected by the situation in which she now found herself. The judge, Mr Baron Cresswell showed little sympathy for the weeping woman before him. He commented on the heinous and dangerous character of the crime of which she had been convicted on her own confession. He told the court that there were many similar instances, where prisoners charged with such an offence were followed by a sentence of transportation for life.

He castigated the prisoner for committing such an act, which he described as being 'none so injurious to society than that of the abstraction of letters from a post office'. He said:

'The feelings of mankind might be sorely distressed from the loss of a letter; the interests of men in a pecuniary point of view might be most seriously affected. For the stealing of a letter containing money

might be the means of interrupting the prosperity, if not wholly destroying the character of the best mercantile house in the country. Therefore, though it is extremely painful for me to pass such a sentence, I feel I should be betraying my duty if I did not pronounce it'.

He then told Sarah Kay that she was to be sentenced to be transported beyond the seas for a term of fourteen years. The prisoner was then removed from the dock sobbing bitterly.

I have been unable to find any transportation records for Sarah Kay in the convict records of Australia. However there is little doubt that she would have been carefully picked for such a responsible position. Perhaps temptation proved too much for her. Without any evidence to the contrary we can only assume that her crime was commuted to the lesser sentence in the Post Office rule book, which was to be imprisoned for a term not exceeding three years. Sadly from this distance in the future, we will never know.

Chapter Five: Mary Ann Clayton.

At a time when women made a living by what ever means possible, there developed a crime known as fortune telling. It had started off as a bit of a parlour game played in the middle class drawing rooms in which a prediction might be made about the name of a future husband. Such games were quite popular and this fact was soon picked up by the lower classes. Suddenly when working class women professed to tell fortunes and began to charge pennies for it, then it was banned. The Vagrancy Act of 1824 outlined its condemnation, and an excerpt from this read:

'Every person pretending or professing to tell fortunes or use any subtle craft, means or device by palmistry or otherwise, to deceive or impose on any of His Majesty's subjects, shall be deemed a rogue and a vagabond'.

One woman who took up this craft wasn't 'evil' in the conventional sense, but she was certainly culpable in that she started a series of events which ended in a young girls death. This was not an isolated instance, as there were many gullible young girls who consulted such people who professed to tell fortunes. Many of them truly believed everything that they were told and treated it as gospel. But this particular Sheffield fortune teller drove a naive young woman to kill herself in the worst possible way.

In 1845 Elizabeth Hewitt was just 18 and she lived with her parents in Wentworth Street, Portmahon. The family were poor and so Elizabeth took in washing to help out with the family finances. At sometime in August she was told about a fortune teller who was supposedly very accurate, and Elizabeth decided to give it a go. Her boyfriend, a young man called Samuel Godley tried to dissuade her, but she would not listen to him. The woman was called Mary Ann Clayton who rightly enough made some quite startling predictions.

She told Elizabeth that she would be leaving Sheffield soon for about two months and on her return her wedding would be arranged, before being called off at the last moment. Finally, but most crucially of all, Mary Anne Clayton predicted that Elizabeth would die from taking poison, some time after Christmas. Elizabeth was not actually sure she totally believed it all in the beginning, but when Samuel invited her to go with him and stay with some friends in Bradford, she readily accepted. The couple got on so famously with the friends that they stayed for a total of eleven weeks.

On their return back to Sheffield, Samuel asked her to marry him and she agreed and delightedly the couple set a date. At some point Elizabeth realised that Mary Anne Clayton's predictions were all coming true, and she began to take it all very seriously as it played on her mind. This was solidified after the date for the marriage was forced to be called off when Samuel's father died. Increasingly the fact that the fortune teller had predicted everything that had happened so far took hold, and slowly Elizabeth came to the recognition that she was doomed. Increasing she believed that fate could not be changed and that she might just as well give in to the destiny that had been predicted for her.

On Thursday 9 January 1845 she bought some arsenic and taking some, died in great agony in the early hours of the following morning. Mrs Elizabeth Hewitt, the girl's mother had noticed that Elizabeth had been very down and depressed for the past week or so. However her daughter carried out her domestic tasks as usual and spent most of the Thursday washing and cleaning the house. She then told her mother that she was going to see her sister who lived in Newcastle Street, Sheffield.
In the latest wash that had been sent to the house, her sister had included some small delicate items, which Elizabeth had promised to wash by hand. However she not got round to washing them and so Elizabeth promised her sister to wash them and deliver them the next day.

She left her sister's house around 5 pm and later she reported that Elizabeth seemed to be cheerful and in good health. The girl was next seen on a place called the White Rails which were situated near an Iron Bridge. She had often stopped there in the past waiting to see her fiance Samuel who worked close by. On this occasion however she met one of his co-workers, a young man called Thomas Allen. The couple stood talking for about 30 – 45 minutes as she asked him how long Samuel would be. Allen told her he would be about another 20 minutes or so and Elizabeth said that she would wait for him.

Meanwhile, her mother, Mrs Hewitt and her husband went to a meeting in the school room attached to the Portmahon Baptist Church. When the meeting was over and they got home around 9.15 pm they found Elizabeth had already gone to bed. Mrs Hewitt went up to see her daughter to ask her if she was ill, and she told her mother that she was not feeling very well and had decided to have an early night. She seemed to be very restless as she lay in bed, tossing and turning and so her mother asked her 'was she in any pain?' Elizabeth told her that she wasn't but she complained of having a great thirst.

Mrs Hewitt got her a carafe of water, but remained concerned as the more her daughter drank, the more ill she became. Several times Elizabeth vomited a great deal. Elizabeth's mother had a grandchild staying with her, and so she told her husband that she would sleep in the little girls bed that night. As it happened that the little girls bedroom was next to her daughters, so she would be nearer if Elizabeth needed her or called out. Subsequently Mrs Hewitt heard her daughter being sick again around 2 am, but then she seemed to be quiet and her mother assumed that she had fallen back to sleep.

Around 3 am a dog's barking woke Mrs Hewitt, and she went again to Elizabeth's room, but her daughter wasn't there. Then she heard a noise from downstairs and went down into the kitchen to find her daughter stretched out insensible on the floor. The poor demented mother called to her husband and together they managed to get the girl back into her own bed. Mrs Hewitt went to make her daughter some mint tea, but when she returned she found her quite dead.

Surgeon Mr Payne was sent for, but there was little that he could do as Elizabeth Hewitt was past all help. An inquest was held at the Acorn Tavern on Shalesmoor, Sheffield on Saturday 11 January 1845 by Coroner Mr Thomas Badger. However, even he admitted that this was going to be one of the most difficult inquests he had ever held. For reasons which he could not explain, Mr Badger experienced some great difficulty in getting the various witnesses to tell the truth. In the end it got so bad that he ended up threatening to have two of them sent to York Assizes on a charge of perjury.

The first witness was Mrs Hewitt who described to the inquest her daughter's sudden illness and death. Then it was the turn of the next door neighbour a Mrs Jarvis. She said that Mrs Hewitt had called her at 3 am and asked her to come next door. She went and found the girl was already dead and had been placed back in her bed by her parents. The witness described how she touched the girls hand and noted that it was still warm. The witness confirmed that she was still at the house when surgeon Mr Payne arrived, and that he seemed totally astonished at the girl's sudden death.

Then the enquiry took on a strange turn as the witness Thomas Allen gave his evidence. He started his testimony by describing the meeting between himself and Elizabeth on the Thursday night. He told the jury that he worked with Samuel at the Hunters Wheel and he had seen Elizabeth who asked him if Samuel had finished work. He told her that Samuel was still at work and the couple stood talking for a few more minutes. He then said that Elizabeth had promised to visit her friend Mary Swift on her way home, who was also Allen's sweetheart.

Allen was also intending to visit his girlfriend and so he went to Mary Swifts house and told her that Elizabeth intended to call in. However he told the inquest that somehow she never arrived. He said he thought no more of it, assuming that instead she must have waited outside Hunters Wheel for Samuel to finish his work. The witness said that Samuel had told him later that he had met Elizabeth after he finished his shift, and the couple had walked into Hillfoot. They had discussed going for a drink together, but in the end they didn't as Samuel only had three halfpence in his pocket. Allen told the coroner that they had both been astonished the next day to hear about Elizabeth's death.

Details of the inquest reported in the local newspapers the next day stated that it had been reported that this witness gave his evidence very reluctantly. The report added that he did not give direct answers to the many questions put to him by the coroner. In the end, Mr Badger told him that:

'it is quite evident that you know more that you are saying, and if you do not tell the inquest the whole truth of what you know, I will hand you over into the custody of the constable'.

After being admonished by the coroner, the witness suddenly changed his story as he seemed to have suddenly recovered his memory. He now admitted that he, Mary Swift, Samuel and Elizabeth had gone to Parvins beer house at Hillfoot on the night that Elizabeth died.

He described how they had all been having a drink and chatting when Elizabeth pulled out of her pocket a small twist of paper, which was tied up at the top with string. The girl told them dramatically 'there's as much here as would send you all home' meaning that there was enough in the twist of paper to kill them all. Then she returned the paper back into her pocket and drank some more of her ale. The witness said that she appeared to be her normal self and quite cheerful, so none of the party paid much attention to her words.

Mary Swift was the next witness and she too seemed intent on hiding the truth. At first she claimed that Elizabeth had pulled out of her pocket a snuff box and a brooch which Samuel had given her. When Mr Badger intervened and reminded her of Allen's statement that it had been a twist of paper that the deceased girl had removed from her pocket, the witness began to look a little abashed. Mr Badger again reminded the witness that she was under oath to tell the truth, the whole truth and nothing but the truth. Then the witness then made the most extraordinary statement that shocked the coroner and the people at the inquest to the core. She said

'I don't know the nature of an oath, or what will become of persons when they die who swears falsely or tells lies. I have never heard of hell, or rewards and punishments. I am twenty two years of age and have never attended any church or chapel in my life'.

Mr Badger was obviously still reeling from the shock of the girls words, as he addressed the inquest and said:

'It is perfectly astonishing that in the present age, with the extended means of education which were everywhere at hand, that there should be found in a town like Sheffield, a young woman aged two and twenty years who knew nothing of the nature of an oath'.

The coroner then patiently explained to the witness the nature of the oath she had made when she took the stand. Mary Swift then changed her story. She said that she remembered that Elizabeth had pulled out of her pocket, what she described as 'a long packet' and said something about it, although the witness claimed that she could not rightly remember what Elizabeth had said. Mr Badger was rightly annoyed as he threatened to have her and the previous witness charged with perjury.

He told the jury:

'I have never in the whole of my experience met with two more unwilling witnesses than the last two. But I am determined to have the whole truth and I will sift the matter to the bottom. I will not issue a certificate for the internment of the body until this enquiry is concluded.'

At this point Inspector Wakefield of the Sheffield police force asked the coroner if he could add something which might explain the discrepancy in the witnesses evidence. Mr Badger gave permission and the Inspector told the coroner that he had overheard the girls father, Mr Hewitt say something to Thomas Allen in his hearing. The officer said that he had overheard the man saying to the young man 'to say no more than he could help, but to tell the truth.'

Mr Hewitt was re-called and questioned, but he denied saying any such thing to Allen. The coroner bluntly told him that he would rather believe the officer than the witness himself. Mr Badger added that it was disgraceful thing for a father to stifle an enquiry into the cause of his own daughters death. The surgeon Mr Payne was asked to make a post mortem of the body of Elizabeth Hewitt before the inquest was then adjourned to the following Tuesday evening 14 January 1845 at 6 pm at the Coroners Office in Bank Street.

At the reconvened enquiry, the first witness was Mrs Jane Hannah Broomhead who said that she was a widow and that the deceased girl had worked for her as a cleaner. However she warned the inquest that Elizabeth often told her untruths, therefore anything she said could not be relied upon. The witness declared that she was aware that the girl had her fortune told and exactly what the fortune teller had said to her. Elizabeth had even confessed to her employer that the whole thing had made her feel very miserable.

The deceased woman's boyfriend Samuel Godley was the next witness and he said that Elizabeth had met him at Hunters Wheel where he worked at 6.30 on the Thursday night. However now he said that they walked towards Hillfoot and on the way she quizzed him as to whether he had taken up with another girl or not. He told her that he hadn't and then he told her to go home as she appeared to have become quite cold whilst waiting for him to finish work. Samuel told the inquest that at last he told Elizabeth that he was going home for his tea around 6.30 pm and said that at that point the couple parted amicably enough.

When one of the jury asked Samuel what frame of mind Elizabeth had seemed to be in at the time, he answered that she did not seem to be in low spirits at all, and seemed to be quite normal as they parted. Asked by the coroner if he knew about her intention to kill herself, the witness claimed that he knew nothing about Elizabeth having bought any poison or intending to use it. Samuel however admitted the incident with the twist of paper had happened, but claimed that it had happened the previous Thursday at Parvins beer house.

He said that like the rest he had not taken her seriously and had just thought that Elizabeth was just joking around. However Samuel disputed some of the other witnesses' evidence. He claimed that he had put off the marriage between himself and Elizabeth, not because of the death of his father, but because he had decided that 'she did not suit him'. His own relatives had said that Elizabeth Hewitt would not make a good wife for him and he had taken their suggestion to heart. Samuel told the coroner that because of that, he had subsequently told the girl that she had better 'look out for someone else'.

Samuel admitted to being very shocked when he first heard that Elizabeth Hewitt had poisoned herself, as he believed that she had done it because of the last words he had said to her. An acquaintance had told him of her death around noon on the Saturday, and he said that he went immediately to her father's house to see if it was true. That's when he found out that it was true and had been concerned about it ever since. Mr Payne the surgeon then gave his evidence and said that he saw that Elizabeth Hewitt was dead as soon as he arrived at the parents house in the early hours of Friday morning.

He examined some powder substance which was on her mothers dress, where she said her daughter had vomited. Just by the look of the powdered substance, he suspected that it could be arsenic. He took a sample home and tested it at his surgery which had confirmed his guess. The surgeon said that he had undertaken the post mortem and found a large quantity of arsenic in the deceased girl's stomach, which was very much inflamed and red. He estimated that the 3 or 4 grains she had ingested would be enough to kill someone.

The Rev Mr Davies of the Portmahon Baptist Church was the next witness and he said that he knew the family well. He told the coroner that he had heard that the girl had her fortune told and that it had made her quite miserable. The coroner decided that after hearing the evidence that it was time to hear from the person most concerned. Therefore he now instructed one of the constables attending the inquest to bring the so called fortune teller before him. There was a moments delay before the woman Mary Ann Clayton, who had been the focus of the whole enquiry was then brought into the inquest room.

She told the coroner that she had lived in Sheffield for twelve years and said that she was a respectable widow who had been employed as a dealer in clothes for the last five years. The woman proudly told the inquest that she was no mere fortune teller, but had a deep understanding of both astronomy and astrology. She also claimed to be able to forecast events by consulting the stars, a craft which she had been taught when she was travelling in Spain and Portugal.

When the coroner innocently asked her if she was a gypsy, the woman retorted angrily that she had never 'travelled with a gypsy tribe.' Mr Badger asked her how she made her predictions and she told him that she could tell the fortune of anyone who knew their date of birth. She said:

'I take a figure from the hour that they were born and I give a judgement from that. I form my judgements from the tenth house of the twelve signs of the zodiac. I find my judgements in books which I have at my house, and which, if necessary I can bring forward. I charge nothing for consulting the heavenly bodies, but if the customer chooses to leave me a sixpence, it is all very well. I can say nothing more'.

Mary Ann claimed that she gave more consultations for free than she ever got paid for, and she was so successful that she did not not need to tout for custom. The witness said that customers wanting their fortune told initially came to her to buy clothing or furniture. As a consequence, she had many people called at her house on Dun Street, Sheffield. The fortune teller claimed that she was so successful that she had many Sheffield ladies of both high class or middle class calling on her regularly. However she said that very rarely would she predict for young servant girls or the like.

Mary Ann stated that she had no private consulting rooms and the readings were usually heard as she and the client sat in her kitchen. The coroner then read the evidence of Mrs Broomhead and the predictions she had made to Elizabeth Hewitt, and he asked her if she remembered the girl. The witness replied:

'La Sir, I never heard of such a thing; I never told any young woman anything of the kind in my life, never. If any young woman comes to consult with me, I give them the best of my judgements and if they take my advice they will never do wrong. I don't keep a book with all the names in who come to see me. I never heard of such a thing. I

never received a sovereign, nor charged so much as a half-a-crown'.

However she did admit to knowing about the death of the young girl, which she had read about in the local newspapers. However she pointed out that there were many other fortune tellers in Sheffield and mentioned four others that she knew of.

The coroner at this point turned to the newspaper reporters who were scribbling away at the back of the room. He said that he hoped the gentlemen of the press had taken down the evidence of this particular fortune teller, in order to expose the proceedings of 'a woman like this'. Then the final witness gave his evidence. He was Constable Jonathon Dearden and he told the coroner that he had gone to all the druggists in the neighbourhood, but had not been able to find the person who served the girl with the arsenic.

After hearing that the coroner Mr Badger concluded the inquest by saying that it was his duty to lay before the magistrates such a case, and he hoped the matter would be taken up and dealt with by them. The jury then retired for just a short while before returning back to the room with their verdict. They declared that 'the deceased destroyed herself by taking arsenic, while labouring under temporary insanity.'

They also added that they too hoped the magistrates would take up the case in order to stop such women as Mary Ann Clayton making predictions and ruining other peoples lives. The inquest was then finally closed and there is no more evidence or mention of Mary Ann Clayton being brought before the magistrates.

This is a most disturbing and difficult case to research, due to the many lies and evasions which the witnesses gave. Were they trying to protect Samuel Godley and the manner in which he had jilted Elizabeth Hewitt. Was that the reason she had killed herself or was it indeed the prediction of the fortune teller? Truth be told I just don't know.

At the end of the day a poor disillusioned young girl, believed what the fortune teller had said and that her fate was inescapable and she took such steps that would end her life. Women such as Mary Ann Clayton had to take some responsibility for the so-called predictions that she made. Whether her intentions were evil, I very much doubt. Fortune telling in Sheffield was a lucrative business as indicated by the fact that four other fortune tellers were all operating in the town at that time.

Chapter Six: Mary Hagin and Ann Jenkinson.

No one suspected that the hearing of an ordinary case of theft brought before the magistrates on Saturday 5 May 1849 would unravelled some of the possibly corrupt practises which went on in Sheffield at that time. The fact that this case involved one of the most respectable Sheffield solicitor's was devastating for him, as it cast doubt on his and his clerks honesty and business practise. It also hinted at some suspected, long standing hostility between the same solicitor and the Mayor of Sheffield.

On that particular morning two prostitutes were brought before the magistrates at the Town Hall. There names were Mary Hagin aged 19 and Ann Jenkinson aged 28 years. They had been charged with a street robbery from a man named Peter Champion on night of Tuesday 1 May 1849. It had been claimed that they had stolen the man's hat and boots and the magistrates, finding them guilty, ordered them to be remanded in custody. However the case took on a more sinister note a few days later on Monday 7 May when the case was heard in front of the Mayor.

The Chief Constable of Sheffield, Mr Raynor told the bench that the two girls had been arrested and charged the day after the crime had been committed. However the police had been unable to proceed any further as they had been unable to find the actual victim, Peter Champion himself. Mr Raynor stated that it would appear that he had been kidnapped by some of the prisoners friends. Mrs Champion the victims wife had told Mr Raynor that she had not seen her husband since Friday, as he had not been home.

The Chief Constable reported to the court that he was pursuing all enquiries into the matter and had heard that very morning that Champion had been seen at Redmire's near Sheffield. Subsequently he had sent some officers after the supposed sighting, but they had not been able to find the man. The Mayor asked that Mrs Champion take the oath and to give her evidence, and she stepped into the witness box. The woman then told a very strange tale. She said that on the morning of Friday 4 May she was at home with her husband, when several men and a woman came to her house.

Mrs Champion stated that one of the men said that they would like to settle the matter about the street robbery the night before, and asked Peter Champion not to go to court and prosecute the case. The woman said that she would give Peter Champion a sovereign to pay for the boots and hat which had been stolen. However the witness admitted that herself and her husband did not know what to do or what the legal consequences might be if her husband did not arrive at court to give his evidence. In the end a compromise was sought and they agreed to go to a public house and discuss the matter.

They all retired to a nearby hostelry and had something to drink which one of the men paid for, but they could not come to an agreement, as the couple maintained their fear of the consequences of a non appearance in a case which they had asked to be prosecuted. So the unnamed women asked them if they would feel better by getting some legal advice, which was agreed. She said that they could consult a well known solicitor of the town called Mr Broomhead. At this revelation all eyes turned to wards Mr Broomhead himself, who it was at that time in the courtroom, as he had been retained to defend the case for the two women, Hagin and Jenkinson.

Continuing with her story Mrs Champion said that she and her husband went to Mr Broomhead's office in Sheffield and one of the men had accompanied them inside. In order to pay for the consultation, the witness admitted that she handed over the same sovereign that the woman had given to Peter Champion to pay for the loss of the hat and boots. Inside the solicitors office was a young man, and Mrs Champion told the court that she presumed the young man was Mr Broomhead himself. So she asked him what the consequences to herself and her husband be, for his non-appearance at court.

The young man simply replied 'There will be no more about it' but then he added more ominously 'however it must not be known that I said so'. With that she claimed that the party left the solicitors offices. The man who had accompanied them into Mr Broomhead's office was aware that she had already handed over the sovereign offered as recompense, had been paid to the young man and so he then asked Mr and Mrs Champion what they would take to make up for the stolen articles. Mrs Champion said at first that a sovereign would act appropriately as recompense.

The man argued that he could not afford another sovereign and he asked her again what she would think was fair. Mrs Champion said that she and her husband had agreed on the sum of 15s. The man offered her 12s saying that was all he had on him, but he could soon get the rest. Then she told the bench she went with her husband to a dram shop in Westbar Green to wait for the man's return. The man left them for a short while, soon after bringing just another 1s, saying he could not get any more.

The witness told the court that by that time it was about noon and she left her husband in the dram shop while she went home to prepare some dinner. Suddenly the witness started to cry as she told the bench that she had not seen her husband again as he had not come home. Mr Broomhead himself then stood up and addressed the courtroom. He said that as this appeared to be a charge against himself and his clerk, Mr Armitage, he asked the bench if he could send for the young man to attend the court. The bench agreed and a constable of the court was sent to summon the young man from Mr Broomhead's office.

Whilst the court waited, the solicitor stated that little reliance could be placed on the words of the witness, as when she had made her first statement she had claimed to the magistrates that she had spoken to him. He said that 'now she is claiming that it was my clerk that she spoke to'. A few moments later the clerk Mr Armitage appeared looking quite flustered. His agitation increased as the woman's statement was read out to him. Mr Broomhead then asked him if there was any truth in the woman's claim, that such a discussion had taken place in his own absence. Mr Armitage replied that there was not the slightest truth in the matter.

Mr Broomhead then turned to the witness and asked her if the clerk she had spoken to, was the same young man she saw standing in the courtroom. Mrs Champion dramatically pointed at Mr Armitage and stated 'that is the person I saw at the office.' The clerk shook his head and stated to the bench that 'that was not the way it happened and the facts are simply these'. He said that he remembered that a man had indeed come into the office with the witness and her husband. Peter Champion had asked his advice as to a non appearance in court. He had simply told him to do what he thought was right and proper.

At this Mrs Champion shouted across the courtroom and interrupted him, saying that he was a liar and that he had told her husband not to turn up in court. The clerk said that her statement was a false one and that he never told the man any such thing. Mr Armitage claimed that it was only when he was taking down the details about the case, did he realise that Peter Champion was prosecuting the case and that it was he that had been robbed. He told the court that he knew that his employer was working for the defence of the two women concerned in the robbery. Therefore he should not even be discussing the case with these people. Consequently he politely asked them to leave.

The Mayor again went carefully over the witness statements, but the clerk said that he had never been asked such questions. The Mayor announced to the court that it was clear that the prosecutor Peter Champion had been tampered with, and the solicitor Mr Broomhead answered 'not by me most certainly'. The clerk stated once again, that when he realised that the husband of the witness was the prosecutor in the case, he told him he had no right to come to the office. Mr Broomhead said that his instructions to his clerk had been simply that when engaged on one side, they should never hold communication of any kind with the opposing side.

The clerk Mr Armitage agreed and stated that is the way he had always practised. When he realised that the man was the prosecutor he was told to go away, and just to do what he thought was right and proper. Mr Broomhead stated his concerns to the magistrates and claimed that no man can be safe if such statements made by 'people such as these who are to be believed over the words of a solicitors clerk'. The Mayor told him:

'I shall act upon the facts that are laid before me, and compel Peter Champion to come here and give his evidence. We cannot allow witnesses to be tampered with under any circumstances'.

He then ordered that the witness be kept in custody, and a warrant made out for the apprehension of Peter Champion.

The following day the two female prisoners Mary Hagin and Ann Jenkinson were once more brought before the Mayor at the Town Hall. This time Peter Champion, who had given himself up was also in the courtroom and he was asked to give his evidence. He told the court that on the previous Tuesday 1 May 1849 in the evening he left his house with 6s or 7s in his pocket. He said that he met up with some friends and they were drinking at several public houses in Westbar up until midnight. Champion admitted that the party ended up deciding to have a last drink in the Bay Horse, but admitted that he was so drunk that he could not remember leaving the public house.

All he knew was that the next morning he found himself at home with his clothes covered in dirt, his pockets empty and his hat and boots missing. Cross examined by Mr Broomhead, the witness confessed that he did not remember seeing the two women the night before and could not swear that they had stolen his boot and hat. Therefore he had decided that he did not want to proceed with the charge of theft against them. The Mayor asked Champion if he had ever been in Mr Broomhead's office and he admitted that he had, the previous Friday.

The witness said that they had gone to the office with a friend of the two prisoners and the Mayor asked him to tell them exactly what had happened there. Champion said that the man with them had a conversation with Mr Broomhead's clerk. When asked if the man was in court, the witness pointing at Mr Armitage. He said that he had a pair of boots and a hat stolen, but that he did not want to proceed with the charge. He had asked the young man that in such a case, would he have to attend the court?

Champion said that the young man had asked him if he had signed anything at the Town Hall when he reported the theft and Champion told him that he hadn't. The witness claimed that the man Armitage had then told him that he was not compelled to appear. However he added that it must not be known that he had told me so, because he must advise persons only what was legal and right'. Once again Peter Champion was asked 'who said that' and he replied 'Mr Broomhead's clerk'. Champion was then asked if that was the reason he had absented himself from home, to which he replied that it was.

The Mayor turned to Mr Broomhead and said 'this is rather strong confirmatory evidence of what was said here yesterday, but the solicitor again stated that no reliance could be put on the man's evidence or that of his wife's. Champion was asked if any money had been exchanged at the solicitors office, and he said a sovereign had been handed over. He also admitted that 13s had been paid to his wife. At this point, the case then degenerated into a polite, but 'through clenched teeth type argument' between the solicitor and the Mayor.

The Mayor claimed that the evidence against the clerk had been confirmed by both Champion and his wife. Mr Broomhead, on the other hand defended his clerk who he said had been with him for ten years and was most respectable and honest. Both the solicitor and the Mayor accused the other of not taking the situation seriously. The Mayor pointed out that anyone who puts his clerk in such a responsible position has to be answerable for his employee's conduct. On the other hand the solicitor claimed that it was a plot designed to injure himself or his clerk.

Angry words were exchanged between himself and the Mayor before the case was allowed to continue. The next witness to give evidence was a man called John Gillott and he told the bench that he was a night watchmen in Sheffield. He stated that he had been on duty in Tenter Street about 1 am on the Wednesday morning when he saw Peter Champion come out of the Bay Horse public house. Gillott said that he saw two men and the two female prisoners following him along School Croft.

The watchman continued with his beat and later saw the four persons who had followed Champion, come out of a darkened road and cross over into Trippet Lane. Gillott said that when he went down School Croft he found Champion laid out on the footpath without his hat or boots. The witness stated that he then called for some assistance from another night watchman called John Ashton, and between them they got the man back to his home. They had recognised the two prisoners and as a result it was around 4 am when he and Ashton went to the house of Benjamin Ward.

They knew that he was the brother of the prisoner Ann Jenkinson. They called out to him to get up and open the door. When Ward opened the door they noted that just inside were a pair of boots, which were later identified by Champion as being his. Continuing with his evidence, Gillott said that he and Ward had then went to a house in Bailey Field where the two female prisoners lived. When he confronted them with the theft of the boots and hat, Hagin had told him that Ward gave her the items.

Jenkinson said that her brother was innocent of the crime, and that she had taken the boots to him and thrown them inside his house without his knowledge. Benjamin Ward was the next witness and he stated that around 1.30 am on Wednesday morning he had been in bed when he was woken up by some rattling. He went to the door and saw two women who said they wanted to leave something at his house. Ward replied that he would have nothing to do with any stolen goods, although he noticed that one of the women threw something inside the door. The witness improbably claimed that he didn't examine the object, but went straight back to bed.

Cross examined by one of the magistrates, he implausibly stated that the night was so dark that he had not recognised either of the women, even though one of them was his own sister. The witness complained that soon after four o'clock he was disturbed again by the night watch and only then did he discovered that it was a pair of boots that had been thrown inside his door. The second watchman was a man called John Ashton and he confirmed that he had been on duty in Bailey Lane on the night of the theft.

He said that by the light of two fires which had been left by some excavation men working on the new town sewers, he saw one of the prisoners carrying a pair of men's boots. He followed them to the house on Bailey Lane and saw them leave the boots just inside. He approached them and asked who the boots belonged to, and one of the woman gave him some cheek. He ordered the two women to go home and then later, hearing that a man had been robbed, he went with Gillott to Ward's house around 4 am where they found the boots. At the end of hearing all the evidence, the two women prisoners were found guilty and sent to take their trial at the next Sheffield Intermediary Sessions.

The Sessions were opened at the Town Hall on Friday 18 May 1849 and the two prisoners, Mary Hagin and Ann Jenkinson were brought before the Grand Jury. They were charged with stealing the hat and boots, but after hearing all the contradictory evidence that had been heard before the magistrates, the prisoners were acquitted and the case was dismissed. Thankfully the Sheffield Police were not to be bothered with Mary Hagin for much longer as in July of the same year she was found guilty of stealing 12 pounds of sugar and ordered to be transported for seven years. Mary Hagin was placed on the convict ship the 'St Vincent' along with another 205 women which left England on 13 December 1849 and landed at Van Diemans Land on 4 April 1850.

The contradictory evidence which was given in the case, suggests a situation of suspicion and possible corruption. It would be interesting to hear what happened, if anything to the clerk when Mr Broomhead returned back to the office, and as to whether he retained his position. It would also be interesting to know if there was any prior 'conflicting history' between the Mayor and the solicitor., Mr Broomhead. Was any further action taken against Peter Champion and his wife? As always, there are no answers, and it was just the two women, both prostitutes and therefore the lowest common denominator that were punished?

Chapter Seven: Maria Woodall.

In 1849 Maria Woodall was aged 18 and she worked as a domestic servant at a chemist's on Fargate run by Mr Horncastle. She had worked there for the past two years, but by the end of December she was applying for other jobs. Consequently at the beginning of January 1850 she started work for the Rev. Mercer, the minister of St Georges Church, Sheffield. According to Maria, she enjoyed the work, but had to leave around the middle of February due to ill health. In reality it seems that poor Maria was keeping a dark secret, like many other poor girls in this book. She was a single woman and pregnant.

It seems that when she started to gain weight it made her mother and sister Catherine suspected she might be pregnant, but Maria denied it. Deeply suspicious her mother went to see a 'water caster' [a kind of fortune teller] called Mr Turton who assured her that her daughter was not pregnant, but that she had developed dropsy. Now assured that her sister was suffering from a form of illness, Catherine took Maria to stay with her for a while in Hull, where she remained for a fortnight in her sisters care. They returned back to Sheffield just in time for Catherine's marriage to a young man named Louis Harworth and Maria then went to stay with them.

Her new brother-in-law was a jeweller who lived in Bright Street, Sheffield and it was not long before Maria assured him that she was now feeling much better and she soon started looking around for another situation as a domestic servant. It was not long before she saw and applied for, a position with a Miss Weaver at Upperthorpe, Sheffield. Maria was invited to attend the house for an interview on Monday 1 April 1850 and Catherine agreed to come with her. However a few days before the interview, Maria was taken ill.

She would not let her sister call in any medical help and said that it would soon pass. Throughout the day she seemed to grow worse, until after dinner, Catherine persuaded her to go to bed. Around 4 pm she heard Maria call out from one of the bedrooms and found her in a state of complete hysteria. Only after some effort, did Catherine succeed in calming her sister, before finally she sent her husband Louis to fetch a surgeon. A nearby man, Mr James Gregory returned back to the house in Bright Street, Upperthorpe and after an examination, he shocked Catherine by informing her that Maria had been delivered of a child.

There was no sign of a child's body and so Catherine demanded from Maria as to where the child was. The girl just shook her head and refused to answer. At that Mr Gregory and her sister searched the room and to their horror in a clothes box found the body of a full grown female child. It had been wrapped in an old skirt and was covered up with more clothes. Upon removing the clothing from around the child, the surgeon found that the baby had been strangled. A piece of black tape, several yards long had been wrapped around the baby's neck and had been pulled so tight that the surgeon was unable to insert a finger under it.

As if to make sure, a piece of material had also been stuffed down the child's throat to prevent it from crying. Mr Gregory showed the child to Maria and Catherine accused her of killing it. Maria just cried and said 'Oh dear what shall I do if I have?' Her sister told her she should speak the truth and pray to God to forgive her. Mr Gregor then tried artificial respiration on the child, even though it appeared to be clearly dead. Needless to say it was all in vain. The surgeon then told Maria and her sister that he had no option but to notify the police and a constable was sent for.

Meanwhile when Catherine asked Maria what had happened, she simply told her sister that she remembered being in great pain, but could not remember anything after that. A constable came and spoke to Maria and he asked Catherine if she knew that her sister was pregnant. She told him of her earlier suspicions and her mothers, but they had been re-assured by a diagnosis of dropsy. The body of the child and the tape that had been around its neck was handed to the constable and he took them away.

An inquest was arranged by the coroner at the Rising Sun public house on South Street, Sheffield Moor for Wednesday 27 March 1850. The surgeon, Mr Gregory was the first witness and he said that from what he could see the baby was born alive and gave his opinion that it had died from strangulation. He described the tape around the child's throat which was so tight that the child would have died of strangulation well before the plug could have been put in its mouth. The surgeon then gave evidence of the post mortem where he found that the child's organs were healthy and the child was full term.

Maria's previous employer Mr Horncastle who attended the inquest at the request of Maria's friends. He told the court that while she worked for him she had been a good and careful servant. However she had several epileptic fits during her employ, and for those attacks she had been treated by Dr Elam who had sent a certificate to the inquest to that effect. Mr Horncastle also told the coroner that the putative father of the child had been one of his assistants, but he had left his employ suddenly, just before the girl herself left to take up her position with Rev Mercer.

The chemist also told the inquest that he was not surprised to find that Maria had been pregnant. He had always suspected a greater intimacy existed between his assistant and the girl than was proper at the time. Mr Gregory then stated that the girl had not recovered sufficiently to give evidence on her own behalf. So the coroner adjourned the inquest to Wednesday 10 April 1850 which was held at the Coroners Office on Bank Street, Sheffield.

Newspapers of the period described Maria as being a good looking girl aged only 18 years who attended the inquest along with her mother and sister. It was reported that she 'appeared greatly distressed on account of her fearful position, and swooned away several times during the proceedings'. The poor girl must have been terrified. It seems that the Chief Constable Mr Raynor had ordered that the girl be accompanied by a woman employed by the police called Jane Osbaldeston who appeared as the first witness.

She told the inquest that she had been with the prisoner since 26 March up to the present time. Maria had shown her great honesty and had told her that she had no recollection of the birth and she also gave her the name of the putative father of the child. The prisoner had said that after she had told the young man she was pregnant, he had given her some dark powder. However they made her so sick that she had not taken any more than one or two of them. Although it had been reported to Jane Osbaldeston that the girl had made no preparations for the birth, the witness had since found a child's cap and two children's undergarments, which were partially made among the girls clothes box.

The next witness was Maria's mother, Alice Woodall and she stated that when she had consulted the water caster Mr Turton she had not been accompanied by her daughter. He had told her that her daughter was suffering from dropsy and given her some drops and told her that all would be well. This statement was confirmed by Mr Turton himself who had sent a letter to the Editor of the *Sheffield Independent* dated Saturday 6 April 1850 which stated that he had not seen the girl and had only discussed the case with the mother. He stated that 'I suspect her own want of care and prudence towards the girl which had led her to endeavour to throw some blame upon other parties.'

After hearing all the evidence, the coroner then summed up the case for the jury and read out the witnesses statements for the prisoner. During the reading of this, Maria was reported as being much exited and her only answer to the charge was that she was unconscious at the time she gave birth. The jury after a short consultation delivered a verdict of wilful murder against Maria Woodall and she was ordered to take her trial at the ensuing Yorkshire Assizes.

On Thursday 11 July 1850, the Assize judge, Mr Justice Cresswell proceeded to discuss the forthcoming cases with the Grand Jury before the trials started. He told them:

'A woman by the name of Maria Woodall was charged with the wilful murder of her new born child. Here the first enquiry for the Grand Jury would be whether the child was born alive, and secondly whether the mother could be supposed to have wilfully destroyed it. If they were of the affirmative opinion they would find a true bill'.

That meant that there was a case to answer and the trial would go ahead. However they discussed the case and they found that there was no bill to answer on the charge of wilful murder but decided, as was quite common in such cases, the prisoner would be tried on the charge of concealment of birth.

Maria Woodall was brought before Mr Justice Cresswell at York on Tuesday 16 July 1850 at the Yorkshire Summer Assizes where she pleaded not guilty to the initial charge of wilful murder. Thankfully she was defended by Mr Overend and Mr Boothby opened for the prosecution and gave the details of the case before the Grand Jury. Mr Boothby stated that in view of their decision he did not think it necessary to offer any evidence. The judge then went on to look into the lesser charge of concealment.

The prosecution, Mr Boothby simply handed the judge a letter from Maria's previous employer Mr Horncastle. Once again he gave her a glowing character reference from the time she worked for him. Mr Boothby stated that the prisoner since leaving Mr Horncastle had worked for Rev W Mercer at Sheffield. However, although he was happy to give her a character, the prisoner had no means to bring him to York in order to speak for her. The judge stated that sentence would be deferred until he had time to consult with some of the other judges at York. Maria, who was showing signs of her distress was then removed from the dock.

On Monday 22 July 1850 Maria was brought back into courtroom for sentencing. It was commented that the girl appeared to be quite stoical as she listened to what Mr Justice Cresswell had to say. The judge stated that he had consulted with some of his colleagues and as a consequence they had agreed that a suitable sentence was for her to be sent to prison for twelve months.

Chapter Eight: Hannah Eliza Glossop.

In this next case, this young woman was judged to be evil, not through any dubious criminal activity, but because she flouted the laws of respectable society. When the object of her affections was a young man claiming to be a doctor, she was doubly damned. In the 19th century there was a lot of respect given to men who were professional doctors, and a lot of resentment shown to 'quack doctors' who were untrained, prescribing medicines and selling so-called 'cures'. Nevertheless much interest was shown at the inquest, not so much in her death, but in her scandalous moral behaviour.

When one such person calling himself Dr Henry went to lodge in Howard Street, he and the married daughter of the house, Mrs Hannah Eliza Glossop became the object of much gossip. That was intensified when she died suddenly in May 1853. At first not much notice was taken, as it was reported that she died from the effects of fever and effusion of blood on the brain. The body was interred and according to the authorities, that was that. However the rumour mills of Sheffield were thrown into a spin when a letter was received by Chief Constable Mr Raynor. The letter alleged that the same Dr Henry had something to do with the woman's death, hinting that poison may have been used.

At first Mr Raynor was reluctant to do anything, but when the Coroner, Mr John Webster also heard similar rumours, he sought permission to have the body of Mrs Glossop exhumed. Consequently the disinterment took place in the churchyard of St Georges Church at 6 pm on Monday 16 May 1853. The coroner had arranged for a post mortem to take place at 6 am the following morning. In charge of the examination were two Sheffield surgeons Mr Wright and Dr de Bartolome and they performed the operation in the presence of five other eminent medical men of Sheffield.

Thankfully no poison was found, but ominously instead, the post mortem revealed that 3 – 4 weeks prior to the young woman's death, she had suffered from a miscarriage and had actually died from puerperal fever. It was suggested that the woman had been within a month of her confinement when the foetus had been ejected, although by what means could not be established. Mr Raynor was told of the results of the post mortem, and he immediately sent for the supposed Dr Henry, who in reality was called Mr Davies. There the man was interviewed and held at the station to await the beginning of the coroners inquest which was due to start later that morning.

The inquest was opened 11 o clock at the Beehive Inn, Glossop Road, Sheffield and the jury was firstly taken to see the body which lay in a coffin at the entrance to St Georges Church. Then they returned back to the Beehive and the enquiry began. Mr Webster stated that the inquest had been arranged, due to a strong rumour about a witness who might have had something to do with the woman's death. That person had not arrived yet, so he announced that he would start the inquest by hearing the evidence from the young woman's mother, a Mrs Mary Simpson. Poor Mr Webster had no idea that the witness would irritate him beyond belief, as she endeavoured to try to paint her daughter and the mysterious 'Dr Henry' in the most favourable light.

The woman who stood to give her evidence was dressed quite respectably, as she took the oath and stated that she was a widow who lived on Howard Street, Sheffield. Mrs Simpson said that the deceased was her daughter, Hannah Eliza Glossop aged 26, who had been married to Charles Glossop a clerk at the railway station. The woman said that since the previous August, both her son and her son-in-law had gone to Australia to find gold. At this point it became clear that the coroner was well aware that some allegations had been made regarding the suspicious relationship between Mrs Glossop and the supposed Dr Henry.

Using cross examination the coroner asked about the relationship between her daughter and her husband and then with the other man. Throughout he called him Mr Davies, his correct title whilst Mrs Simpson always referred to him as Dr Henry. Mrs Simpson told him that Dr Henry had come to lodge at their house two years previously. Then the conversations proceeded along these lines:

Coroner: 'Was there not some unhappiness between your daughter and her husband?'.

Mrs S: 'Not a bit. It was a love match. They ran away to get married, and there was never a more affectionate couple'.

Coroner 'Had he ever expressed any jealousy of Mr Davies and his wife?'

Mrs S: 'No, he idolised his wife too much for that. My daughter and her husband and Dr Henry used often to walk out together.

Coroner: 'Has he ever, to your knowledge given anything to your daughter, such as any medication'.

Mrs S: 'I don't know that he ever gave her any medication of any kind.

Coroner: 'Have you observed any considerable intimacy between your daughter and Mr Davies.'

Mrs S: 'Nothing more than if her husband had been at home.'

Coroner: 'Have you not known them stay out late at nights together – till twelve at night or one o'clock in the morning?'

Mrs S: 'Oh no'.

Coroner:'Have they not been out late at night together?'

Mrs S: 'No they have not. They have gone out a good deal together, but not at all against my wishes. He frequently took her and her child out in the gig, and I have gone with them too'.

Coroner: 'What time have they returned when they have been out together?'

Mrs S: 'Never late, because we are never out of bed later than 12 o clock. My daughter had a miscarriage in August last, a fortnight *before her husband sailed for Australia, and she has never been well since'.*

Mrs Simpson said that since the miscarriage eleven months earlier, her daughter had been attended to by a surgeon Mr Barber. He had also attended to her more recently from Monday 2 May right up to her death on Tuesday 10 May at 8 pm. The woman stated that the following Friday she had been interred at St Georges Church alongside her father's grave. Mr Webster bluntly asked Mrs Simpson if her daughter had a miscarriage since her husband went to America, but she again denied it angrily. She agreed that her daughter had been ill, but claimed it was simply by exerting herself with too much packing for her husband and her brother for their trip.

At this point the coroner was informed that Mr Davies had arrived at the inquest accompanied by the Chief Constable, Mr Raynor. The man who was, by now the object of much of the speculation regarding the young woman's death, was brought into the room. Mr Webster was well aware that the man's real name was Alfred Davis and he and his two brothers, one in Sheffield and the other in Manchester used the professional name of Henry & Co. Therefore Mr Davies always introduced himself as Dr Henry. However on this occasion he was accompanied by two local solicitors, Mr Fretson and Mr Fernell.

They politely asked permission from the coroner to attend the inquest and to ask questions of the witnesses, to which Mr Webster gave his assent. Only then did he address the jury and open the inquest officially. He told them they were there to enquire into the death of Mrs Hannah Eliza Glossop, who had died on the 10 May and had been buried on 13 May 1853. Then he gave the jury the reasons why the death and burial of this young woman had come to the attention of the authorities in Sheffield. He told them:

'In consequence of great irregularities at the internment, where it had been reported that several of the parties attending the funeral were very tipsy. One of the pall bearers was exceedingly ill-used and another was sent to the Town Hall. There was a regular fight

and it was thought that one of the parties would have been killed, in consequence of the most disgraceful conduct.'

He concluded that several communications had been sent to him and also to Mr Raynor imputing that the death of Mrs Glossop was due to some act or deed of Mr Davies, with whom it was said that 'the deceased had long conducted herself with some levity.'

Mr Webster went onto explain that the two people had lodged together in her mothers house on Howard Street for some time. To the disgust of the neighbours, the pair were in the habit of going out together and staying out until the early hours of the morning. The coroner stated he had no intention of casting aspersions on a deceased person, but that was the reason why her husband had separated from her and gone to Australia, simply because of his wife's immoral conduct. There had also been an allegation that the young woman had been poisoned.

In consequence of such information being received, he felt it his duty to order the body to be disinterred and an examination made to establish the real cause of death. Throughout his statement Mr Webster was continually being interrupted by Mrs Simpson until he rudely told her 'you had better withdraw Madam, or not interrupt me'. She then put on a display of solidarity with Mr Davies that infuriated the people in the inquest room. She openly went to the other end of the room to where Davies was sitting, and put both hands on his shoulders she kissed him on the cheek.

The coroner was clearly sickened by this display and he called a woman called Mary Hattersley to be the next witness. She introduced herself as having nursed Mrs Glossop up to the night previous to her death. She said that for the few days before the woman's death, she could not get the deceased woman to eat or drink much at all. However she added that her patient had taken a little wine and brandy as prescribed by Mr Barber. When asked by the coroner why Mrs Glossop had not eaten much, the witness added that she was unconscious for most of the time.

Mary Hattersley said that following a visit from Dr Barber and Dr Bartolome, they had ordered a blister to be put on the back of the patients neck, which she did. Sadly she told them that coming back later in the day, she found Mrs Glossop to be in a dying state. The witness told the jury that when she was asked to nurse Mrs Glossop she had not previously visited the woman at her home, although she knew of her by sight. At the end of her evidence, one of the solicitors who had accompanied Mr Davies to the inquest Mr Fretson, then asked permission to speak to the mother of the deceased woman, Mrs Simpson, which was granted.

Under his careful questioning the woman admitted that she had identified the body of her daughter after the exhumation. Mr Fretson also asked her what was her daughters relationship with Mr Davies. Mrs Simpson once again replied that her daughter had gone out with Dr Henry on several occasions, and he had always asked her permission before doing so. The woman claimed that she herself had often fixed her daughters bonnet and got her things ready to go out with him 'many a time.'

The next witness was a woman called Ann Camm who told the jury that she too was a nurse and had gone to the house in order to dress the blister for Mrs Glossop, and that she had still been in the room when the poor woman died. She told the inquest that as she left the house, that a man had spoken to her called Mr Clubb, who was the first person to make the allegation that Hannah Eliza Glossop had been poisoned by Mr Davies. Mr Fretson asked who he was, but curiously the witness said she did not know, although she seemed to have known his name.

However the coroner pointed out that this statement was hearsay and could not be taken as evidence, and Mr Fretson concurred, but pointed out that it would be helpful if they could speak to him and take his statement. The coroner asked the Chief Constable if they could trace the man, to which he said that he would try. Then the garrulous witness said that she had often seen the deceased woman out with Dr Henry several times, and they had even been away together for a week or a fortnight on holiday.

Surgeon Mr M Bartolome was the next witness and he gave evidence of being called to see the deceased on Monday 9 May with surgeon Mr Barber. He stated that he had found the patient labouring under considerable irritation of the brain and slipping into and out of an incipient coma. Because of this she was unable to speak. He said that her symptoms were such that she could not move out of bed, and he deduced from these symptoms that bleeding was taking place in her brain. The surgeon said that she was quite insensible at times and both of the pupils of her eyes were dilated.

In consultation with Mr Barber, the two doctors had ordered a blister to be placed on the nape of Mrs Glossop's neck, but he admitted that he never held out any hope that she might recover. He said that in questioning the mother of the girl, Mrs Simpson she told him that her daughter had two miscarriages. Once when she attended the Great Exhibition in London two years previously, and another a fortnight before her husbands departure for Australia. However she had described her daughters present illness as merely being a fever on the brain.

Mr Bartolome admitted that her explanation of the recent illness seemed to fit his examination of the woman and therefore he did not examine the girl as minutely as he should have done. He also admitted to having seen the woman out with the man calling himself Dr Henry and 'like others I had seen them out at all hours'. He added that it was the talk of the neighbourhood for months past. Mr James F Wright then gave his evidence, as he told the jury that he had conducted the post mortem as ordered by the coroner. He stated that in this examination he had been accompanied by several surgeons of Sheffield namely Dr Bartolome, Mr W Jackson, Mr Lewis, Mr Porter, Mr G Atkin and Mr Herbert Walker.

He gave a long description of the conditions of the body's organs before concluding that his opinion was that the uterus had lately contained a foetus which had been expelled not earlier than four to six weeks previously. The coroner tried to get him to decide whether the foetus had been expelled normally or whether an instrument had been used, but the surgeon would not commit himself. However since the suspicion of poison had been mentioned to him, he suggested that the contents of the stomach should be analysed.

Dr Bartolome was the next witness and he concurred with his colleague's conclusions. When he too was asked if he thought the foetus had been expelled normally, he could not say, as he had found no injury in any of the woman's parts. He suggested that the inquest be adjourned until the stomach had been analysed, but he said that would not interfere with the cause of death which was a coma induced by intense congestion of the brain.

A hairdresser called Henry Norton who had been called to shave Mrs Glossop's head, stated that he had seen the man Davies administer to the woman in the bed, some white mixture from a bottle which a servant had brought into the room. Mr Raynor admitted that several bottles of medicine had been removed from the house, and that he held up one that had some white mixture in it. He handed it to the hairdresser who smelled at it. He was asked if that was the same white mixture given to Mrs Glossop, but the hairdresser shook his head. He said that the white compound had smelled of sweet nitre but that didn't, as he handed it back. At this point Mr Davies admitted that the medicine was his own which had been prescribed by Dr Gregory.

The coroner now stated that he would like to ask Mr Davies some questions himself and asked him to introduce himself. The man gave his own name and said he was a patent medicine proprietor. The coroner immediately asked him 'are you a regular qualified practitioner' to which the witness was forced to answer that he wasn't. Mr Webster asked 'are you a member of any college?' and again the answer was in the negative. The witness explained that he was part of a firm called Henry and Co who had practised for the last 14 or 15 years in Manchester. At that point Mr Webster announced that he was adjourning the inquest to the following Tuesday to be held at the Town Hall.

When the inquest was resumed in the evening of Tuesday 24 May 1853 by Mr Webster, it was noted that because of all the publicity and the notorious nature of the case, the room was overcrowded.

The first witness was a servant at the house on Howard Street called Mary Bamforth. She told the inquest that she had been in service with Mrs Simpson for more than five years, but had left five months previously. When asked the reason for her leaving, she said that since Mr Glossop had left for Australia she had frequently seen 'improper familiarities between Mrs Glossop and Mr Davies.'

When the coroner asked her to expand on that, she listed having seen Mrs Glossop sitting on Mr Davies' knee, lay her arms on his shoulders and kiss him. The witness also said that there had also been an incident when the couple were locked in the bedroom together after lunch, and she had been asked to make the bed up afterwards. A member of the jury asked if she had ever seen Mr Davies give any medicine to Mrs Glossop, which she denied. She too agreed that the deceased and Mr Davies had been out late together, although she could not recall if they had ever stopped away all night.

Surgeon Mr J Barber stated that he had attended the deceased from the 3 May to her death and he had made out the certificate of death. He said that during that period of treatment, he had not considered that the fever she had suffered from was puerperal, but since the post mortem he had since changed his mind. He gave the reason for this as being on the first consultation, the answers given by the patient and Mrs Simpson led him to the conclusion that the girl was suffering simply from a fever. However he admitted that knowing that her husband was away, he did not think it necessary to make a personal examination of Mrs Glossop.

He now believed that he had been deceived by them both. He had prescribed some white mixture, which contained spirit of ether. Mr James Heywood a professional chemist told the inquest that he had analysed the stomach contents of Mrs Glossop, but found no vegetable or mineral poison. However he said that he would not have expected to find anything which might have been administered weeks before the woman died, that might have been given with the intention of bringing on an abortion.

A curious conversation then took place between the coroner and Mr Davies which were questions as to whether or not he had previously lived in York, to which the witness admitted that he had. However he would not answer the coroners question as to how long he had lived there, stating that it had nothing to do with the present enquiry. It seems evident from the questioning that there had been some suspicious activity from Mr Davies in York, which might be related to questions around whether or not he had been accused of bringing on an abortion.

Then Mr Davies made a curious statement when he said:

'It was publicly reported that I left Sheffield in consequence of the young woman dying. I did leave Sheffield on the Tuesday morning [the morning before Mrs Glossop died] but it was in consequence of some business I had to conduct. I have nothing further to say.'

The coroner summed up for the jury, telling them that was all the evidence he had to bring before them. They consulting together for 30 minutes before returning a verdict that:

'The said Hannah Eliza Glossop died from a coma, arising from intense congestion of the brain and inflammation upon its surface, consequent upon her having recently been delivered of a foetus. But whether by natural or artificial means, there is not sufficient evidence to prove'.

The foreman of the jury, a Mr Booth who was a grocer of Church Street, Sheffield stated that the jury were concerned about the 'loose behaviour' exhibited by Mrs Glossop before she died. He asked that 'the jury beg to express their strong opinion as to the impropriety and levity of conduct, not only of Mrs Simpson and her late daughter, but also of Mr Davies.' The enquiry was then closed.

There we must leave the mystery surrounding the death of Mrs Hannah Eliza Glossop. Surely the only fault that could be ascribed to the young woman, was to flaunt her relationship with a man who was clearly a fraud and a charlatan. Her foolish mother, no doubt charmed by his bogus medical title encouraged her daughter to a degree, where she became the subject of a public scandal. As a consequence they tried to cover up her relationship with a man suspected of committing abortions, possibly from which as a result, she had died.

Chapter Nine: Sophia Tomlinson.

In Victorian society, as we have seen from the previous case, immorality was much frowned upon, particularly in the case of women. In February 1863 this violent case came to the public's attention in Sheffield not so much for the murderous crime committed by a woman, but for the history between the two women which had provoked the attack. On the face of it the two women had much in common, as they were both of the same age, in their twenties and both married to chimney sweeps of the town. However when jealousy rears its ugly head, it can only end in one outcome.

In February 1863 a quarrel broke out between two women in Willey Street, Sheffield. The protagonist was called Sophia Tomlinson and she attacked Emma Allen with a small but very sharp knife. In fact the two women had been friends once upon a time, and had even shared a house together on Willey Street, along with their husbands. However it was what had happened during that period that had led to jealousy between the pair, and which had led to a murderous and frenzied attack.

In the evening of Monday 9 February Sophia stabbed at Emma's head with such viciousness, that she inflicted some deep and serious wounds before she could be stopped. The incident had happened so quickly, that even though it was a busy Sheffield street, it took a minute or so before the two women could be parted. Even as she was dragged away from her opponent, Sophia kept slashing at Emma, trying to inflict as much damage as she possibly could. The surgeon Mr Sykes was called in to attend to the wounded woman and found that from the amount of blood that she had lost, and the deepness of the wounds, that she was in a very serious condition indeed.

Sophia Tomlinson was arrested and the next morning she was taken before the magistrates charged with cutting and wounding Emma Allen. The prisoner told the court that she lived with her husband in Edward Street, Sheffield. The hearing was just a short one as the Chief Constable of Sheffield, Mr Jackson simply asked for a remand in order that the police could continue with their enquiries. He also stated that Allen was unable to attend the court due to her injuries, and that it would be at least another week before she could appear to give her own evidence. The magistrates had no option but to agree and a remand was granted.

Thankfully by Saturday 14 February 1863, Emma had recovered sufficiently to appear, and she entered the court with her head swathed in bandages. She told the bench that she lived in Willey Street, on the Wicker and admitted that the two couples had all got on so well together that they had all lived together. Some months previously however an argument had ensued and the four people had separated with the prisoner and her husband going to live at a house in Edward Street, Sheffield. Then she came to the real reason for the sudden attack.

It seems that Sophia husband had gone to Emma's house on Willey Street on both the Sunday and Monday in order to see a cousin who had been taken ill and was staying at the house. Sophia, not surprisingly given the nature of their previous relationship at that house, had objected to this. When one of the magistrates questioned why she should object to this, the crux of the stabbing soon became clear. It seems that the two women had swapped husbands at one point and as Emma tried to explain the situation to the bench, Sophia interrupted her statement in the courtroom and said 'she lived with mine first.'

Emma told the court that Sophia's jealousy was unfounded as on both days she was occupied reading to the invalid as he lay in bed. In fact she claimed that she had never spoken to Sophia's husband, who remained downstairs with her own husband talking in the kitchen. On the Monday evening she was standing in Willey Street talking to a young girl called Mellon, when Sophia approached them. Very quietly she asked Emma if her husband had been at her house and was he there at that moment? Emma told her that he wasn't at her house, and that she didn't know where he was.

Sophia then called her a whore and said she would make her know and to Emma's horror drew out a small carving knife that she had been hiding in her clothing. Emma began to run, but her attacker soon caught up with her and stabbed her several times in the forehead and breast, before she could even begin to defend herself. The witness described her attacker as acting quite demented, so ferocious had been the attack. Emma told the bench that at that point she fainted and some people who had gathered around in the street, had carried her to her home.

The girl, Harriet Mellon confirmed the fact that she had been talking to Emma Allen on Willey Street when out of the blue she was attacked by a woman from behind. The witness told the court that she remembered seeing the sudden attack, as the prisoner pulled the knife out from her dress pocket where she had been keeping it. The girl admitted to screaming at the onslaught, and as a consequence several people had gathered around.

Surgeon Mr Sykes described being called to the house on Willey Street after the attack in order to attend to the injured woman. He noted as he arrived that she was bleeding copiously and that the patient had already lost a great deal of blood, which was on her clothes and all down the front of her dress. He said she had four or five deep wounds on the forehead, of which three had gone down to the bone. He then described her wounds in more detail.

He said that the woman had several puncture wound on her breast. One of which was about half an inch in length. She had a three small wounds on the top of her head which were quite deep, and finally that she had a large scratch on her neck which looked like it had been made by fingernails. He stated that the wounds were all very serious and he still had concerns as to whether she would recover completely. A witness to the attack was a man called John Styring who lived on Wicker Lane, told the court that he had seen the prisoner lunge and attack the woman Emma Allen.

The witness described how he had immediately run up to the two women, and had tried unsuccessfully to get the knife away from the prisoner. Despite the fact that he held her by her shoulders, she still manage to inflict several wounds on the other woman before he could wrest the knife out of her hands. The knife was then produced in court and the witness identified that it was the same knife that he had removed from the prisoner. He then related how a constable was called and Sophia Tomlinson was taken into custody.

The prisoners defence solicitor, Mr Clarke Branson tried to point out that Sophia had suffered much provocation from her attacker, but the chair to the magistrates stated that 'such cases could not be treated summarily.' They then discussed the case between themselves before finding the prisoner, Sophia Tomlinson guilty. The chair to the magistrates ordered her to take her trial at the next Assizes. The magistrates concluded that the conduct of both the woman were considered 'far from irreproachable.'

On Monday 9 March 1863, in opening the Yorkshire Assizes the judge, Mr Justice Keating made some remarks to the Grand Jury. He commented on the large numbers of cases to be tried before them and he said that he had observed 'an anomaly in many of the crimes the jury would hear'. Justice Keating told them that the state of the country was quite prosperous at that time and that he had noted the prevailing crimes were those which reflected those times.

He said that most of the crimes committed by the 103 prisoners they were due to try, had originated from 'foul passions of lust, revenge and malice'. He must have been referring to cases like that of Sophia Tomlinson who was brought before him the following day. The prosecution Mr Blackburn opened the case and outlined the events for the jury. He described the fact that both woman had been guilty of 'a disgusting piece of immorality, the prisoner living with the prosecutrix husband and the prosecutrix living with the prisoners husband.'

Mr Blackburn told the court that peaceful state of things had ceased by 9 February and he described the events leading up to the attack. Sophia Tomlinson who was undefended, just shook her head when asked if she had anything to say. The jury lost no time in finding her guilty and she was sentenced to eight months imprisonment.

Chapter Ten: Elizabeth Charlton.

In the nineteenth century most working class, pregnant women chose to be attended by a local midwife, rather than pay the costs of a trained and qualified surgeon. Many of these women, had little knowledge of the childbirth process or the need for hygiene. More often than not their only qualifications were that she had given birth herself or had attended to numerous others. This naturally offended the fully trained and qualified doctors, who had spent years practising their skills. One of the most dreadful of these was a woman from Attercliffe called Mrs Elizabeth Charlton who, even though she was responsible for one woman's death, went on to kill another.

It all started on Thursday 16 September 1863 when the Coroner, Mr J Webster Esq., was forced to hold two inquests on the same day The first was on the body of a 33 year old married woman names Mrs Squires who had died in childbirth and the second was a druggist called Harvey Oakes who had committed suicide to avoid a charge of improper treatment. It was known that Mrs Squires had previously given birth to several children, when, on Tuesday 8 September 1863, she had been seized with labour pains. As previously arranged, she called in the midwife called Mrs Elizabeth Charlton and the first baby was delivered safely around 10 pm.

The midwife knew that the baby was one of twins, but instead of urging the mother to continue pushing, in her ignorance as the labour pains had now ceased, Elizabeth actually allowed her to remain for twelve hours in that condition. At 10 am the following morning, Wednesday 9 September, instead of calling in a qualified surgeon, the midwife called on the services of Harvey Oakes who kept a chemists shop in the High Street, Attercliffe. He was also known to assist at births and advertised himself as an accoucheur [a male midwife]. After examining Mrs Squires Oakes told her that the baby was a cross birth, which meant that the foetus was lying with neither the head nor feet facing the birth canal.

Instead of turning the foetus into a position where birth could be achieved, he gave Mrs Squires two powders to induce the labour pains once more. When nothing happened and after the druggists had several 'tots' of brandy, he proceeded to try to move the child manually. Instead of the child going into the correct position for birth, all that happened was that he caused the poor mother excruciating agony. After many hours of this torture, she screamed out to Mrs Charlton 'do not let that man touch me again'. Her husband hearing his wife's cries, simply put Oakes out of the door. Thankfully a qualified doctor, Dr Shaw was quickly on the scene, and he delivered the mother of the, now dead child, in five minutes.

Sadly, the poor mother, already weakened by the prolonged labour and the rough treatment she had received at the hands of Oakes, sank into a very weakened state. Puerperal fever set in and she died a week later on Tuesday 15 September 1863. As the knowledge of the rough treatment by the midwife and particularly that of Oakes became known in the neighbourhood, much anger was expressed and he found himself the object of many scathing remarks. On Wednesday 16 September he had become aware that an inquest had been ordered to enquire into the death of Mrs Squires. Hearing this he became very agitated, and convinced that his reputation was now in ruins.

The following day he got up around 6 am got a small bottle of prussic acid from his chemists shop and returning back to his bed, he swallowed it. On a sheet of paper that was found in his room Oakes left a note which read:

'Hunted like a dog and being innocent of the villainous imputations about to be sworn against me, is more than a mortal man can bear. God bless my mother; God bless my brothers and sisters; God bless my dear wife and children'.

In the corner of the paper, having run out of room he had scribbled 'and may heaven have mercy on me'.

The first inquest was held on the body of Mrs Squires, and the first witness was William Squires the husband of the deceased woman. He told the coroner that his 33 year old wife had gone into labour and the delivery of his first child, one of twins was successful. The baby was alive and said to be a fine healthy one. However the midwife Mrs Charlton had experienced some problems with the delivery of the second baby and around 10 am on the morning of Wednesday 9 September, she asked him to fetch Mr Oakes.

Subsequently he called in at the chemists shop on his way to work and passed on the message. William Squires then said that he then went to conduct some business, however when he returned and heard his wife's cries during the pummelling she received at Mr Oakes hands, he became very concerned. William told the coroner that his wife said that she wanted Mr Oakes out of the room and begged him to 'leave her alone' but the druggist would not go. Hearing this, Mr Squires 'discharged' him forcibly, and banned him from ever coming to his house again.

A neighbour who was also at his wife's bedside, urged the witness to contact Dr Shaw the surgeon, and he went to his house and asked him to come back with him to attend to his wife. He told the surgeon that his wife had said that the man Oakes 'had killed her'. He readily admitted to the coroner that like many men of the times, he did not enter the bedroom whilst his wife was undergoing her labour, but simply waited anxiously downstairs. Mr Webster asked the witness if Mr Oakes was drunk when he saw him, either at his own shop or later whilst dealing with his wife.

Mr Squires said that the man did not appear to be drunk, but he did not seem to know what he was doing. When William was asked why he had not called in a surgeon to his wife in the first place when she first went into labour, he replied that it was his wife who had made the arrangements to call Mrs Charlton in, and he had nothing to do with the matter. Later after seeing the man in the street, Mr Squires told him that he would pay his fee, but he was not to go anywhere near his wife again.

A neighbour of the deceased woman called Mrs Woodhouse then gave her testimony and confirmed the details about sending for Oakes and his treatment of Mrs Squires. At one point she admitted that she could barely watch him manhandling the pregnant woman and she quickly left the room. In the end her friend and neighbour begged her 'not to let him touch her again' and that was when she asked William to send for Mr Shaw. Once he arrived and took over, and the dead baby was delivered almost immediately.

Finally the moment which the observers at the inquest had been waiting for took place as the midwife Mrs Elizabeth Charlton was then sworn in. She was described as being 'an old woman' but who had surprisingly 'only practised as a midwife for a year in Attercliffe'. Elizabeth went through the evening and described the rough way in which Oakes had dealt with Mrs Squires. Also asked by the coroner if she thought that the man Oakes was drunk, she replied that although Mr Oakes hadn't seemed to be drunk when he arrived, but she had witnessed him drinking some of the brandy that was already in the room.

It was only when she saw him pulling and pushing at the woman, did she realised that he did not know what he was doing. Mr Webster closely questioned her about her experiences as a midwife and she told him that she had never attended the birth of twins before. However she understood that the mother should be allowed to rest after the delivery of the first child, if there were no labour pains. The next witness was the father of Dr Shaw who had attended to Mrs Squires. He introduced himself as Mr George Shaw who worked at St Bartholomew's Hospital in London and had delivered many baby's there during his time.

Due to his reputation as a qualified doctor who had specialised in midwifery, he had accompanied his son in undertaking the post mortem on the deceased woman. The surgeon stated that in his opinion she had died of puerperal fever and he found that the placenta was only partially removed. Dr Shaw said that the deceased woman was excessively weakened after the prolonged labour and the rough treatment she had received. The eminent surgeon concluded that in his opinion the fever would probably have been induced by the retention of the placenta.

He added that the powders which the midwife had given Mrs Squires would have done nothing at all to induce labour pains, as the child was not in a proper position to give birth. At the end of his evidence the coroner asked him 'would you also say that the course which was taken by Mr Oakes could be called malpractice, and the witness relied 'decidedly so'. He then gave his opinion that if the child had been turned into the proper position, which would have taken just a few moment if undertaken by a professional man, the baby would have been born immediately, and the remainder of the placenta would have been expelled.

The fact that it wasn't done so had resulted in excessive shock and weakness to the woman's system. Dr Shaw added that the midwife also did wrong by waiting 12 hours after the birth of the first child. There should have been nothing to prevent the birth of the second child, twenty minutes or so after the first. The jury at this point unanimously expressed their opinion that the midwife was clearly to blame. Mr Webster then summed up for the jury. He told them that when he first read the details of the case, he assumed it would be a clear case of manslaughter against Harvey Oakes, if he had lived. However he had changed his mind after hearing about the incompetence of the midwife.

He advised the jury that if they wanted to return a verdict that this woman died of puerperal fever brought on by the improper treatment of the midwife or Harvey Oakes, it would meet the justice of the case. The foreman of the jury stated that they felt that the midwife ought to be severely censored for her neglect. Sealing the woman's fate, the surgeon Mr Shaw added that the fact that 'she says she has never attended a twin birth before, which is something I find incredible, and I cannot consider a midwife knows her business who has never attended a twin birth.

The coroner then address Mrs Charlton herself and told her that the woman's death was brought on 'and rendered more dangerous from your ignorance of the duties of a midwife, and from the bad treatment of Harvey Oakes'. He told her that both himself and the jury felt that she was much to blame, or almost as much to blame as Oakes had been, 'because your actions in allowing the woman to wait for twelve hours was contrary to all reason'. He warned her:

'For the future be a little more careful, and if you have any doubt as to the consequences, send for a surgeon, a properly educated man and he will use all that skill to put things right. Under any circumstances that second child ought to have been born alive, within twenty minutes of the first.
You ought to know better that to allow a man like Oakes to treat the woman in that way; and I hope you will take this as a warning. This woman came to her death in a very cruel manner. I hardly know how to find words strong enough to express my feelings, but there is no doubt she died from gross ignorance of yourself and Harvey Oakes. We cannot censor him, he has censored himself'.

In disgrace, the midwife Mrs Elizabeth Charlton was then allowed the leave the inquest room.

The jury then proceeded to hold the second inquest into the death of Harvey Oakes. After hearing all the evidence, they returned a verdict of suicide during temporary insanity and the inquest was closed.
It might seem that after being publicly censored by the coroner for her involvement in this crime that Mrs Charlton would never have practised her art as a midwife again. But unbelievably, not only did she carry on, but just three months later was again involved in the death of yet another young, pregnant woman from Sheffield.

When a single, unmarried woman called Ellen Athorne became pregnant later that year. For reasons that were never fully explained, she demanded that no one be at the birth except for herself and the midwife, Elizabeth Charlton. Ellen had lived with her mother in a yard off Carlton Road, Attercliffe and on 29 November 1863 she gave birth to a still-born child. After the birth, the poor girl fell into a fever and lingered until the 15 December at around 11.45 pm when she died. An inquest was called by the Coroner Mr John Webster at the Sportsman Inn, Attercliffe on Thursday 17 December 1863 and the jury was sworn in.

Their first duty was to see the body of the deceased woman at the home which she shared with her mother. When the jury returned back to the public house, the girls mother was the first to give evidence. Mrs Sarah Athorne told the coroner that she had given birth herself to 14 children and that her daughter was the eldest and she would have been aged 21 the following March. She said that the father of the dead child had been a man called Jonathon Parker. She described how she realised that her daughter was having a difficult birth, even though the midwife kept assuring her that her daughter would be fine.

After the baby was born dead, the family doctor, Mr Davidson was finally called in, and he was appalled at the way in which the midwife had dealt with the young woman. Mr Davidson told her that 'the midwife had almost destroyed her daughters insides'. The distraught mother told the jury that the midwife had drank a good deal of wine whilst attending to her daughter, but had little to eat, during the long hours of labour. She said that it had lasted from 8 am to 8 pm. Mrs Athorne said that she had witnessed the midwife give her daughter two powders, although she did not know what it was for.

In reply to a juror she told them that she had wanted the same local surgeon, Mr Shaw to attend to her daughter, but the girl had refused to have anyone but Mrs Charlton. Only when she was dying on 15 December did the girl admit to her mother that she should have followed her advice. Asked by the coroner if her daughter had ever complained about her treatment at the midwives hands during the hours of her labour, Mrs Sarah Athorne denied it. At that point Mr Webster told the jury:

'The investigation cannot now proceed any further without a post mortem examination of the deceased. Because charges had been made against the midwife, Mrs Charlton, and those charges being very heavy and serious, it is necessary for her own protection. It was also necessary in order to ascertain the real cause for the young woman's death, and therefore such an examination should be made'.

The coroner stated that he had therefore asked surgeon Mr Walker of Sheffield to conduct the post mortem and to report back to the reconvened inquest. Mr Webster, clarified that he had not asked the family doctor Mr Davidson to undertake the post mortem, as 'the official complaint about the midwife had originally come from that gentleman'. So he had decided that it would be better for all concerned to have an investigation by an impartial surgeon. The coroner then openly condemned the fact that the women of Attercliffe should persist in employing unqualified midwives 'after the sad instance of want of skill, that some of them had lately shown'. Then he adjourned the inquest until the following Monday.

When the inquest was re-opened, two aunts of the deceased called Maria and Ann Hurst, and her sister-in-law Mary Ann Athorne, also gave evidence of attending to the girl during her lengthy labour. All three relatives stated that they had been with Ellen from the beginning to the end of her confinement. They all agreed that the labour had lasted from an early hour and it had been a very painful and drawn out one. Although the two aunts had left before the baby was actually born, they said that although Mrs Charlton did her duty as far as they could tell, better assistance should have been found.

The girls sister-in-law, Mary Ann Athorne said that she had stayed with Ellen after the aunts had left and the baby had been born with in a few moments of them going. She stated that there were no signs of any violence on the baby when it was born, however the midwife had 'pulled the child about 'pretty middling during the delivery'. The deceased woman's sister-in-law confirmed that before the birth, that no one could persuade Ellen to have any other midwife but Mrs Charlton. She had since found out the woman had persisted in boasting that 'she could deliver any child without any surgeon being in attendance at the birth'.

The next witness was the surgeon Mr Herbert J Walker who had undertaken the post mortem on the girls body. He told Mr Webster that he had found the girl to be a strong, sound young woman and all her vital signs had been healthy. He stated clearly that death had resulted in severe and extensive inflammation of the ligaments of the bladder and womb and a displacement of the latter. This had been followed by mortification, which had progressed so far as to make it impossible to tell precisely what injury had been done to the young woman. He gave his opinion that with qualified assistance, the birth might have been a difficult one, but the girl could have been delivered with perfect safety.

Mr Walker told the inquest that he had no hesitation in attributing the case to malpractice on the part of the midwife. At this point the midwife herself came into the inquest room to gave her evidence and for the second time in her life, all eyes were upon her. Mrs Charlton told the inquest that about 30 minutes before the birth, she had given the girl two powders of ergot of rye mixed with some gruel. She claimed that the reason for giving the girl this was because at that at that point, she realised the baby was dead. Nevertheless she knew that despite this, the baby had to be delivered and she gave the girl the powders for that purpose.

As she was saying this, the surgeon Mr Walker intervened and stated that ergot of rye was used in the birth process, but it was not considered by qualified doctors to give it in first cases. Mrs Charlton continued with her statement and denied using any violence, although she realised that the girl was in severe pain. Once again Dr Walker stated his disagreement with the witness and said that he had no doubt that the injury and consequent inflammation, mortification and death were brought on by the use of her extreme force. He added that the effect of ergot of rye would increase effects of the force on the woman's body.

Mrs Charlton concluded that she had attended many first births and that she had only done what any doctors would have done before her. Dr Johannes Davidson the assistant to Mr Shaw was the next witness and he said that he had attended the deceased from the Tuesday after her confinement to her death. He stated that in conversation with the midwife, he had found her to be ignorant of all the 'niceties in midwifery practice upon which the success and proper care of the patient depend'. Dr Davidson said that he had noticed the woman's injuries on first attending to her, and he concurred with the previous witness. He too stated that death was caused directly by the violence she had suffered at the midwife's hands.

Dr Davidson then listed all the woman's internal injuries which he had found when he first attended to her, before sealing Mrs Charlton's fate when he told the inquest that the womb and the bladder had been torn apart. He stated that:

'I could not undertake to say that the deceased would have lived if she had proper medical attention from the first; but I will say that the actions which caused her death were violent and for which there was not the least occasion, and which ought never to have been used. I never before saw such an extensive injury; it is quite impossible that a woman so injured could recover'.

Mrs Charlton once again tried to explain why she had given the ergot of rye, but the coroner interrupted her explanation, by informing her that what she ought to have done was to call in a skilful surgeon.

Mr Webster then summed up for the jury distinctly laying the blame for Ellen Athorne's death on the midwife. He stated that in his opinion any midwife who displayed such a lack of skill was quite unfit to attend confinements. However he said that it was for the jury to decide whether there was negligence on the part of the accused. They had to decide whether that negligence would amount to manslaughter or whether the natural difficulties of delivery should excuse her by returning a verdict of death from natural causes. However the coroner pointed out that after hearing the evidence of Dr Davidson, they would have little difficulty coming to that decision. He told them:

'I should say that she had certainly not shown competent skills and knowledge in her chosen craft. The case is a very serious one, not only as regards the deceased woman and her offspring, but as regards society. For if midwives totally ignorant of their duties are allowed to act in this way, we must expect to have many more deaths. With these observations I will leave the matter in your hands'

The jury after a brief consultation returned a verdict of manslaughter against Mrs Elizabeth Charlton. She was told by Mr Webster that she would be committed on his order to take her trial at the next assizes. Its was reported that she was then removed and lodged at the cells in the Town Hall until Tuesday 22 December 1863 when she was allowed bail.

Elizabeth Charlton was brought before judge Mr Justice Byles at the Yorkshire Spring Assizes on Tuesday 29 March 1864 charged with the manslaughter of Ellen Athorne. The case was outlined by the prosecution Mr Waddy, and he described the prolonged labour that the young woman suffered. The witnesses once again gave the same evidence as had been given to the coroner, before the defence Mr Vernon Blackburn spoke. He stated that the prisoner had only taken the same steps as would have been completed by the most skilful surgeon, before claiming that the woman would probably have died anyway.

He also suggested that the case held an element of medical jealousy of a female interfering in an area which should have been the province of male surgeons alone. He also claimed that the investigation had been instituted out of a sense of disgust because the person who assisted at the birth had been a woman. Incredibly given the woman's history of neglect and malpractice, after just half an hours consultation the jury brought in the verdict of not guilty and Elizabeth Charlton was discharged.

Chapter Eleven: Bridget Finnerty.

This case is quite shocking in that it gives us an insight into the absolute poverty of life in Sheffield during the nineteenth century. Living in such squalor often resulted in people finding some kind of oblivion through alcohol. We already know that children's lives were held very cheaply, during this period, even by their own parents. However when a mother is addicted to drink, the result for the children is inevitably neglect, starvation and death.

The Sheffield authorities first became aware of the Finnerty family in October 1869 when the body of a three week old little girl, also called Bridget Finnerty after her mother, was found at home of her parents on Sunday 10 October. The house was rented by Bridget and Michael Finnerty in a court off Bailey Street, Sheffield. Police enquiries proved that on Friday 8 October the three week old little girl had been taken to several public houses by her mother. On returning back home that night, whilst intoxicated, Bridget claimed that she had accidentally knocked the child's head against the table edge, inflicting a bruise from which, two days later she died.

An inquest on the child was held on Thursday 14 October 1869 by Coroner Mr J Webster at the Green Seedling Inn also on Bailey Street. The first witness was the mother Bridget who identified the body of her child, and told the inquest that her daughter had started to convulse around 2 am on the Tuesday morning and had died almost immediately. The coroner asked her about the mark on the child's head, and Bridget told him that on the Sunday, two of her older children were quarrelling and she went to hit the oldest one and missed her, and hit the baby instead knocking her head against the table.

The Chief Constable told the court that the mother Bridget had a history of drunkenness and had been in front of the magistrates three times all together. When one of the magistrates asked the mother why she took a child so young out with her at night, she claimed that she was breast feeding the baby and so when she went out to the public house, she had been forced to take the child along too. Bridget said that on Monday she had gone to the Fox and Ducks public house and had some glasses of beer. Then later she had called in at another pub called the Crystal Palace where she remained until almost midnight.

Following another question from one of the jury, as to what other people felt about this, the witness said that several people had asked her if the baby was alright, and she always told them it was fine. The coroner asked her how many children she had and Bridget told him five, but only two of them were still living. Mr Webster was clearly disgusted with the woman, as he said to her:

'There is no doubt that the child has died through negligence. If a woman gets drunk when a child is three weeks old, it will help to kill it. I think if we cant punish you, your own mind will'.

Mr Robert J Walker surgeon said that he had undertaken the post mortem on the child and found no signs of violence except for the mark on its head. However ominously he stated that there were no sign of food anywhere in the child's body. The mother had told him that the baby had suffered from convulsions before it died, but internally there was also no signs of convulsions on the brain. However Mr Walker added that the child might have been in such a weak condition through ill feeding and through sheer neglect, that might have been having convulsions from which there was now no evidence.

A midwife Mary Miller was the next witness and she said that she had attended to Bridget during her confinement. She admitted that the child had been very weak when it was born, and that she had witnessed it having convulsions soon after birth. The midwife said she had seen the little girl a week previously and she looked very ill indeed. The jury returned a verdict of 'died from natural causes, aggravated by the gross neglect on the part of the mother'. Bridget was called back into the room and the coroner castigated her for her neglect of the three week old child. He did not mince his words as he told her:

'We think the child has been grossly neglected, but we are not able to punish you. We have reason to believe it is from your drunken

habits and keeping the child out at night, taking it to public houses and elsewhere, which has hastened its death. If you are brought to the Town Hall again on a similar charge, you will not get off with a small fine, but will perhaps be sent to prison.'

The coroner must have been quite prescient as five years later Bridget Finnerty was again responsible for the death of another child.

In January 1874 Bridget and Michael Finnerty were still together and were lodging in a house in Royal Oak Yard, Hollis Croft, Sheffield. It was one of the poorest lodging houses in Sheffield and had only three rooms. Living in the house in total were eleven persons, so it was terribly overcrowded. The couple lived in one room along with their four children who were aged seven, six and three and the youngest was called John who was just five months. The couple were so poor that they had few bits of furniture and had to share their bed with their children.

Little John slept on the side of the bed nearest to the wall and next to his mother and father. The three smaller children slept at the bottom of the bed. Unsurprisingly Bridget had resumed her drunken ways and on the night of Monday 19 January 1874 she was brought home drunk once again. It seems that on that night she had been drinking with two cousins in a public house on Bailey Lane for some hours. Subsequently she had been brought home by them at 11.30 pm. Police enquiries established that the father Michael was not entirely sober either, and had some drink which sent him almost immediately to bed, where he soon fell fast asleep.

He woke at sometime around 7 am and went to relieve himself before climbing back into bed and falling asleep again. He woke about 10 am and got up and went downstairs leaving his wife and children in bed. Soon after his wife joined him in the shared kitchen and she got him something to eat before he left to go into town. Later that day he noticed Bridget walking along Hollis Croft and he noted that she was not wearing her bonnet, which was most unusual for the period. When he returned home around 8 pm he found two women who were neighbours in the house. They had gone inside earlier to find the other children crying and John dead in bed.

The police and the coroner were notified and an inquest was arranged on the body of John Finnerty on Thursday 22 January 1874 at the Royal Oak Inn on Hollis Croft. Michael Finnerty was the first witness and he told the Coroner Mr D Wightman that he worked as a moulder. He described the events of the last few days, before the coroner asked him what wages he received. He told him generally it was about 30s a week and out of that he gave Bridget 22s – 23s a week. Mr Wightman asked him how many children he had and Michael told him three living and four dead.

The coroner then asked him if any inquests had been held on any of the children that had died, and Michael looked rather shamefaced as he said that one had been held about five years previously. He offered the information that his wife had neglected the children and the youngest had died. The witness then related how he had returned back to the house to find his wife missing and the two women there. One of them had told him that Bridget had gone to visit relatives at Bradfield, but when he made enquiries about her, they had not seen her.

Michael said that he had not seen his wife since he last saw her walking along Hollis Croft without her bonnet. The landlord of the lodging house was a labourer called James Gerratty and he told the coroner that he had given the couple notice to quit due to Bridget's riotous, drunken behaviour and he described the many occasions when the police had been called to his house because of her. The landlord said that on Tuesday 20 January Michael had gone out about 10.30 am and his wife had not come down into the kitchen around 11 am.

Gerratty, being aware that the couple were under notice, asked her if she had found other lodgings yet. She said that she had and shortly afterwards left the children and walked out of the house and the landlord said that he had not seen her since. Gerratty explained that he had gone into Sheffield himself to try to find her, after realising that she had abandoned her children. He had tried several of the public houses she had been known to frequent, but had not succeeded in finding the woman.

He was aware that Bridget's children had nothing to eat and told one of the older children to bring the baby downstairs, so that his wife could feed it, but when the girl returned she told him that John was asleep, but she didn't think he was breathing. Two women then went upstairs and found the child dead. Gerratty told the coroner that both Finnerty and his wife drank, but she always drank to excess. She would go out drinking and leave the children without food. Consequently they were sometimes fed by other people in the house out of pity.

Mr Arthur Hallam, the police surgeon stated that he had completed a post mortem on the child and found it in a greatly emaciated state. He said that there was scarcely any fat on the child and no trace of food in the stomach or intestines. The liver and kidneys were extremely congested as if they had been pressed upon and the brains and lungs were bloodless. He believed the child had died from syncope [exhaustion] accelerated by want of food and neglect. One of the jury added that he had often seen the woman carrying the child through the streets of Sheffield at night, and often the child had no clothes on and was in a state of perfect nudity.

The coroner was obviously disgusted as he addressed the jury and summed up the evidence for them. He told them that:

'I cannot see how a woman could treat her children in this abominable way without being criminally liable. This is the second child whose death had been caused in the same family by neglect. It is your duty to use the most urgent means in your power to put an end to such a state of things. If a case like this was passed over without sending the woman for trial, I think the office of coroner and jury to be a complete farce and useless.'

Mr Wightman said that his own conclusions were that someone had to be responsible for the child's death and someone had to be sent for trial. The question for the jury was whether it should be the man or his wife. After a short consultation the jury agreed that Bridget

Finnerty was guilty of the manslaughter of little John Finnerty and she was committed on a coroner warrant to take her trial at the Leeds Assizes. Before he left the inquest room the coroner severely censured Michael Finnerty for his own neglect of the child.

Local newspapers of the period reported that the Sheffield police were urgently searching for the woman Bridget Finnerty, but she was not found until two weeks later. She was arrested and brought before the magistrates on Friday 13 February 1874 charged with the manslaughter of five month old John Finnerty. The terrible poverty in which they lived was reported in the *Sheffield Independent* dated Saturday 14 February 1874. The report stated that:

'The case showed a dreadful state of social wretchedness and depravity. The father and mother of the deceased were always drinking and rarely went to bed sober. The place they lived in was extremely dirty, and four children slept in the same bed as themselves'.

The prosecution in the case was Mr Clegg and he described how the couple had consistently ignored and neglected their children. He said that on the very last day they were together as a family 'without feeding any of the children, the man went to work and the woman went out and never returned'. The magistrates after listening to the evidence, again adjourned the case in order that the mother could be found and her evidence taken. However when the case re-opened on Wednesday 18 February 1874, although Bridget was there, very little new evidence was heard.

Bridget Finnerty had been charged with the neglect of her children to which she pleaded not guilty. The police surgeon, Mr Hallam was asked to clarify what he termed as 'neglect' and he said that in this case it was the inattention of the mother, not only by neglecting to give the child and food, but also in leaving the child alone and uncared for. He concluded therefore that the child had not died from any organic disease, but from a simple want of food. After hearing this the magistrates found the prisoner guilty and she was committed to take her trial at the next assizes.

Bridget appeared at the Leeds Spring Assizes on Wednesday 1 April 1874 in front of judge Mr Baron Pollock. The judge in consulting with the Grand Jury before the case was heard, had said that 'with regard to the manslaughter cases, several of them ranked in that savage class of cases which were all too familiar'. In particular he noted the case of Bridget Finnerty and referred to it as 'a very solemn and painful case'. He claimed that there was reason to think that the woman was in a condition of poverty, but it had been alleged in her defence that she was not always aware of the condition of the children.

He argued that the woman therefore was not guilty of absolute negligence which would make her criminally responsible for the death of the child. Mr Baron Pollock explained that the woman had not deliberately ignored the child purposely, and he warned the jury that 'there was a difference between positive wilful neglect and carelessness arising from want of judgement'. The jury returned a verdict therefore of not guilty and the prisoner was accordingly discharged.

I find the judges conclusions very difficult to follow as far as his reference to the woman who 'seemed to be not always aware of the condition of the child' unless he was implying some form of learning difficulties. It is very difficult to deduce the truth in many cases due to the poor reporting of the facts, but surely the two children died because she seemed to be always drunk.

I suppose it was possible to deduce that in such a state Bridget Finnerty might not always be aware that she had not fed the child or the other children, but in my eyes she was still culpable. The father, Michael seems to have been held to be completely exonerated from all charges, but my feelings are that he was equally as guilty as his wife.

Chapter Twelve: Mary Truelove.

On Thursday 27 October 1870 a 41 year old woman called Mary
Truelove was brought before the stipendiary magistrate Mr J E
Davies Esq., at the Sheffield Town Hall. She had been accused of
the attempted murder of her husband Joseph. The couple had lived
on Allen Street, Sheffield and her husband was a pen and pocket
knife forger. The bench were told by the Chief Constable, Mr
Jackson that the prisoner had stabbed him in the neck as he slept. He
said that there had been some concerns that the woman showed
signs of insanity, consequently he said:

*'She had been examined by the police surgeon, but at present I
could not say whether her mental condition was caused by what she
had done, or whether she was really insane. I would therefore like a
remand in order that she can be under my care for another day or
two'.*

Mr Jackson added that due to the fact that Truelove was still in
hospital on account of the terrible injuries he had received, therefore
he was unable to attend the court in order to give his own evidence.
The magistrates agreed that the woman was be remanded until the
following day. It was hoped that by then her husband would be well
enough to attend the court himself.

Accordingly the following morning the injured man was helped into
the courtroom where he still appeared to be in a very weak and
fragile state. Truelove was given a seat from which he was allowed
to give his evidence, as his wife Mary covered her face with a
handkerchief. It was said that the woman appeared to feel great
remorse on seeing the results of her moment of passion. Truelove
told the court that they had been married for twenty years the
previous Christmas, but for the last few years they had been most
unhappy together. The witness claimed that as a result they had slept
in different bedrooms, which he reasoned was due to his wife's
frequent and uncontrollable drinking habit.

The injured man related how the previous Wednesday evening,
around 12.30 am he had gone home to find the door to the house on

Allen Street locked and barred against him. He shouted and banged on the door, and eventually Mary came and opened it. Pushing past her, Truelove said he was going to bed. However instead of going into her own bedroom, to his surprise, his wife lay down on the bed beside him. There she just talked and talked at him until he at last fell asleep. Truelove related how, even as he was falling asleep, she was still talking at him.

Suddenly he felt a stab in his neck with some sharp instrument, which at first Joseph thought had been a razor. He immediately jumped off the bed and found that he was bleeding from the neck. Still clutching at his neck with bloody fingers, he saw Mary leave the room and he heard her going down the stairs and out the front door. The witness told the court that he called out for help, but he claimed it would be half an hour before any help arrived. That was only when he saw a neighbour Robert Riches dressing himself across the road, as the windows of the two houses were so close together.

By shouting across to him, Truelove finally managed to gain the neighbours attention and Riches came to his assistance around 5.30 am. The neighbour called for a cab in order to get the injured man to the Sheffield Infirmary, where the house surgeon immediately attended to his wounds. Joseph Truelove told the court that he had been in a very weak condition and at first the hospital surgeons had feared for his life, due to the amount of blood that he had lost. At this point the stipendiary magistrate, Mr Davies asked the witness if he had been intoxicated himself when he went home. But the witness admitted that although he was not exactly sober, he knew what he was doing.

When the prisoner was asked by the magistrate if she wanted to ask her husband any questions, she said that when they were talking together on the bed he had been very rude to her. Mary told the court that he had refused to let her sleep with him, and instead had called her a foul name. Continuing with his account, Truelove related that their marriage had been anything but a happy one. He said that he had often returned home from work at night to find the house empty, and Mary was out drinking in some of the pubs of Sheffield.

Truelove reported that, as a consequence, he had often been forced to go and bring his wife home from many of the public houses where he usually found her. The magistrate asked him if he considered himself to have been a good husband and the witness said that he was. He claimed that he had always given Mary part of his wages and as a result she had never wanted for anything. At this point the prisoner intervened and accused her husband of not giving her any money for the last 15 weeks, which he denied.

The magistrate Mr Davies then asked him if he had always set a good example to his wife and the witness said that he had always been a good husband to her. Mr Davies then asked him where had he been, if he had not returned home until 12.30 at night. Truelove replied that it was not usual for him to stay out late, but on this occasion he had got into company with some friends and hadn't realised what time it had been. Then the magistrate came to the crux of the real reason for the animosity between the couple. He asked the witness straight out, if he had charged his wife with adultery with two other men, and reluctantly the witness admitted that he had.

The next witness was the neighbour Robert Riches who told the court that he was employed as a carter, and that he lived in the house next door to the couple. He related hearing his neighbour shouting out 'murder' and when he went to the window Truelove said that his wife had cut his throat with a razor. Riches said that upon hearing this, he had hurriedly dressed and went next door, but found the door locked. So he put his shoulder to the door and managed to break inside. There the witness said he found Truelove coming down the stairs with blood pouring out of the wound in the right side of his neck. His shirt and clothes were already soaked in blood and he seemed to be on the point of collapse.

The neighbour said he called for a cab and whilst waiting, he went upstairs and found a pair of bloody scissors lying on the pillow of the bed. Riches related how he had gone back downstairs and showed them to the prisoner, who identified them as ones his wife used which were usually kept in her sewing box. The scissors were produced and shown to the court and it was reported that they were a formidable weapon, being about a foot in length. At this point Mary again interrupted and she asked the neighbour to confirm that he had heard the injured man threaten to have her put in an insane asylum.

Riches was obviously discomforted to admit that he hadn't heard any such thing, but Mary was not going to let him off that easily. She demanded that he tell the court how her husband came home at all hours of the night, and when he did there was generally an argument. Riches shrugged his shoulders and said that he could not say. Then Mary asked him if he had heard that her husband kept a razor under the pillow with which he had threatened to cut her throat, but the witness just shook his head and said that he had heard no such thing.

Police Constable Harvey of the Sheffield Police force was the next witness and he told the court that after the attack, the prisoner had gone to the police station in order to give herself up. The officer said that when he had heard what Mary Truelove had to say, she was taken to the cells whilst he went to the house to investigate. There he found the injured man and he accompanied him to the Infirmary, listening to his account on the way. By the time he got back to the police office, he told the prisoner 'Mary Truelove I charge you with stabbing your husband' The prisoner replied 'It is right, is he dead? If he is not, I hope he is.' At this point the magistrate remanded Mary Truelove until Monday in order that the court would be able to hear the medical evidence.

When the court reconvened again in front of Mr Davies on Monday 31 October 1870 the first witness was Mr Arthur Hallam the house surgeon at the Infirmary. He stated that when Joseph Truelove was admitted he was in a very weakened state due to the loss of blood. The surgeon said that he found the man's wound in his neck which had been about two thirds of an inch deep. Mr Hallam related that it was thankfully at the back of his neck and therefore had not been as serious as it might have been. He said the weapon used was a blunt one and when shown the scissors, the house surgeon admitted that they were the likely weapon used.

Inspector King of the Sheffield police told the magistrate that the prisoner went to the police office around 5.20 am in order to give herself up. When he spoke to her she appeared to be very excited and he asked her what had happened. Mary Truelove told him that she had just stabbed her husband in the neck with a pair of scissors, and that she hoped that he was dead and not suffering. She admitted that she had been drinking and had called in at a public house called the Strong Arm for a rum on her way to the police station.

Inspector King told the bench that the prisoner had then handed over the key to the house and he had, in turn sent PC Harvey to check out if the details the woman had given him were true. The prisoner seems also to have heard the rumours about her state of mind. She said 'they will say that I'm out of my mind but I'm not. I knew exactly what I was doing'. At that point the magistrate asked Mary Truelove if she had anything to say. The prisoner told the court 'its no use sending me to an asylum, because I shall not go.' The magistrate Mr Davies told her there was no question of that, but he also told her that 'you are charged with stabbing your husband with the intention of murdering him'.

The prisoner admitted 'Yes, I did' and Mr Davies told her that they would send her to take her trial at the next assizes. It would seem that there had been some reports that the prisoner had a history of insanity. However as the *Sheffield Daily Telegraph* dated Tuesday 1 November 1870 made clear, there was little evidence of this in the magistrates court. The reporter stated that the prisoner 'was very orderly in court and answered all the questions put to her with extraordinary deliberation'.

Mary Truelove appeared before the Leeds Assizes on Tuesday 6 December 1870 in front of judge Mr Justice Byles. She pleaded guilty to stabbing with intent to murder her husband Joseph. The judge tried to get her to change her plea to 'not guilty' of the crime, but Mary insisted that she was guilty and she refused to change her plea. The prosecution stated that on the night of the incident that both parties were the worse for drink, and in the course of an argument her husband Joseph Truelove had accused her of being too familiar with other men.

A barrister acting for Truelove told the court that he had been instructed to say that his client had no vindictive feeling against his wife and had no interest in pursuing the charge. After hearing all the evidence, the jury gave a verdict of guilty before the judge addressed the prisoner. He told her:

'Mary Truelove mine is a very painful duty. Two or three days ago I went as far as I could, or as I thought I ought to do, in inducing you to retract the plea of guilty. Now you stand convicted on your own confession of stabbing your husband. My sentence can be but this, that you be kept in penal servitude for the term of your natural life'.

The prisoner was then removed to the cells beneath the court room to begin her sentence. Did she regret her insistence of being guilty, sadly we will never know. One thing for sure she would have had many years to regret her actions of that night and the particular irony of her married surname.

Chapter Thirteen: Annie Bishop.

In the next case there is yet another case of a man being stabbed by a woman, as well as an illustration of how even the simplest argument can swiftly turn to murder once a knife is involved. So common were these cases of stabbings becoming in Yorkshire, that the judge at the Leeds assizes noted that there were eight cases of women attacking persons with a knife, in that particular Calendar of Felons. He condemned it as a growing menace.

In the early hours of Sunday 27 October 1872 a twenty eight year old file cutter named John Worthington was on his way home. He lived in Mount Road, Parkwood Springs, Sheffield in a house he shared with his wife and three children. Worthington had just been having a night out at the Alexandra Music Hall in the town and had really enjoyed the performance. So much so that around 11 pm he had called in to see his parents who lived in Pea Croft and told them all about the show. As he related the funny exploits he had seen at the theatre, he little suspected that this would be one of the last days he had to live.

Worthington left his parents house around 11.30 pm and then headed for the home of a friend called Philip Fisher, who lived in what was referred to in the press as 'a low quarter of the town' an area called Smithfield. The court where the Fisher's lived was typical of its time. It was described as being like a square with several houses built around and a pump in the middle. Worthington was describing to Fisher and his wife about the nights entertainment, when suddenly there was the sound of a disturbance outside. The couple's 14 year old daughter Rosina came into the house and complained that neighbour Annie Bishop had called her a bad name for no reason at all.

Fisher immediately went outside to ask the neighbour what was the matter, and why she had called his daughter a bad name. As he went outside he found yet another argument had broken out and quite a crowd was gathering in the yard. After a minute or so his friend John Worthington joined him. The two men stood for a moment watching what was thought to be initially a row between neighbours.

Suddenly voices grew louder and soon, in front of their eyes both men and women were fighting and pummelling each other.

Fisher's wife had also followed them outside and she too stood amazed at the crowd of people now arguing and pushing at each other. It seems that originally the argument had been between a 30 year old woman called Annie Bishop and a neighbour called Charlotte Goodison, during which, it was reported, some incredibly bad language had been used by the two women. One of the neighbours later said that she had heard Bishop shout out that 'she was ready to fight anybody'

Suddenly Annie Bishop ran into her own house, and Fisher's wife advised the neighbour, Goodison to go back inside her own house, which she did. When Annie came back outside, now brandishing a knife and found her assailant missing. She immediately turned on Mrs Fisher and began abusing her for interfering. Fisher then heard the woman's husband David Goodison shout out that the prisoner had a knife in her hand, and Fisher turned around and instructed his daughter, Rosina who was stood at the door, to go back into the house.

Fisher then asked Annie why she had called his daughter a bad name and he pushed at her. She later said that he had struck out at her. As this happened, Worthington went over to defend Fisher when without any further provocation the woman lunged at him, and he found that she had stabbed him in the stomach. Looking down Worthington could see blood coming from the wound and at that he collapsed and had to be carried back into the Fisher's house. Fisher at this point had his back to the court and was making sure his daughter was safely inside the house.

He heard the scuffle behind him and then saw his friend Worthington going back into his house and he followed him, not knowing at this point that the man had been stabbed. Only when his friend turned to face him inside the house. did he see his awful injury. Worthington was put to bed in a fainting condition. as by now his bowels were protruding from the stab wound. A doctor was called, but was unable to attend and so a cab was ordered to take the badly injured man to the hospital.

Fisher, who accompanied his friend, heard Worthington urge him and another man who was with him to prosecute Annie Bishop as he claimed 'it was her and her alone who had stabbed me'. Worthington was quickly admitted into the Sheffield Infirmary and the man and woman named Annie and Henry Bishop were arrested and charged with assault. It was decided at that point by the police and legal authorities that given the serious condition of John Worthington, that the man's dying deposition would need to be taken. In order to do this a Justice of the Peace, named appropriately as Mr W K Peace went to the Infirmary with the magistrates clerk.

Both prisoners were also escorted to the ward in the custody of Police Constable Smelt. They were taken to the bedside where the injured man lay dying. A defence solicitor who had been engaged by the magistrates, Mr Fairburn was also present on the prisoners behalf. The injured man was placed sitting up on pillows in order to give his evidence. Worthington stated his occupation and address before describing the events that led up to the attack. He stated that he knew that he might not survive and that he had been involved in a fight outside the house of his friend Philip Fisher. He also confirmed that he had been stabbed by the female prisoner.

Mr Peace asked him if he had known the woman who had stabbed him, previous to the attack and he told him that he knew her by sight, but had never spoken to her before. Mr Fairburn asked him if he was sure that it was the female prisoner who had stabbed him, as he had described the court as being crowded with both men and women. Worthington told him distinctly that although the night was dark, most of the doors in the court were open and so, although it was night time, the court was brightly lit. He confirmed that he was not mistaken in his attackers identity as he pointed at Annie Bishop. His statement was taken down and Worthington added his signature to the bottom.

The two prisoners were brought before the stipendiary magistrate Mr J E Davis Esq., on Tuesday 29 October 1872. Annie Bishop was charged with the actual stabbing and Henry Bishop charged with aiding and abetting her. An account of the attack was made for the bench by the Chief Constable, Mr Jackson before Mr Fairburn applied for bail for the male prisoner. He pointed out that the deposition made by the injured man, had not implicated the man in the crime, but Mr Jackson opposed this application. The magistrate pointed out that in view of the serious condition of the injured man, he did not feel justified in granting bail at that point. Sadly, later that day John Worthington died of his injuries.

An inquest on the body was held by Deputy Coroner Mr D Wightman at Sheffield Infirmary on Wednesday 30 October 1872. The first witness was the deceased man's father James Worthington who stated that he had identified the body of his son. The man was obviously still distraught, as he told the jury that his son was married and the deceased youngest son and his grandchild was only three years of age. He was followed by Philip Fisher who described the evening of the attack. He admitted that the female prisoner was very drunk and that before the struggle, that her husband was trying to get her back in the house to prevent any trouble.

However Annie Bishop was not a woman who would be told, and throughout the evening she had been challenging various other people to fight. Another witness, David Goodison also described that attack and told the inquest that when he heard the row, he saw the female prisoner run across the court with a knife in her hand. He called out a warning, but it was only later that he heard that a man had been stabbed. However when cross examined, Goodison admitted that he hadn't actually seen Annie Bishop stab anyone and he hadn't seen her husband Henry at all.

Fishers daughter Rosina gave her evidence and said that she had seen Annie Bishop drop the knife after the stabbing. She said that she had bent down to pick it up, but the female prisoner angrily snatched it away from her. When it was time for her father Philip Fisher to give his evidence, he was asked by the coroner whether there had been any animosity between the Fishers and the Bishops before the attack. He admitted that his brother Charles had been in a fight with Henry Bishop a few weeks previously, when he had called his wife a bad name.

The witness continued with his description of the night of the stabbing and said that when he saw the state of his friend, a local doctor was sent for. However he was unable to attend, so the witness said that he got a cab and with the help of another friend got the injured man to the Infirmary. On the way there the deceased man seemed to have a presentiment that he would die very soon. He urged his friend to ensure that the woman Bishop was to be prosecuted, for he declared that she had been the one to stab him.

Cross examined by Mr Fairburn, Fisher denied giving Annie Bishop a black eye, during the argument, stating rather it had been inflicted by her husband before the attack, after he had tried to unsuccessfully to get her back inside the house. Mr Arthur Hallam, the house surgeon at the Infirmary said that the deceased had been admitted around 1 am on the Sunday morning, and he remained in a very serious state until Tuesday when he died from peritonitis. The surgeon confirmed that it had been brought on by the wound to the abdomen.

After the witnesses had all been heard, the coroner summed up for the jury. Mr Wightman told them that:

'they must decide how the deceased came to his death, as it has not been fully proved by the evidence that it was the female prisoner who stabbed the deceased, although you might fairly assume that it was the case. If you believe that she did stab him, there are only two courses open to you, either to return a verdict of wilful murder or manslaughter against her. The law does not require that malice should be proved in order to enable a verdict of wilful murder to be returned, as malice is assumed.'

However the coroner warned them that they must also take into account the type of weapon used, as any person carrying a knife would in all likelihood use it, and in that case the verdict should be wilful murder. After just a short deliberation the jury returned a verdict of wilful murder against Annie Bishop, and the coroner issued an order for her to take her trial. On the next day the two prisoners were brought before the magistrates, when Mr Fairburn succeeded in getting bail for the male prisoner, Henry Bishop. However the magistrates ordered that the sureties were to be set at the high price of £50.

As was usual when the judge, Mr Baron Piggott discussed the cases with the Grand Jury before the assize trial started, he referred to the case of Annie Bishop. He said that from what he understood from the depositions, there had been some fighting in the court and during the fighting the prisoner received a black eye and her husband was knocked down and injured. When Worthington came out of one of the houses, she was seen to run up to him with the knife in her hand, although no one saw the blow being inflicted. Therefore, he stated there was no direct evidence against the prisoner as being the one who actually inflicted the blow.

Mr Baron Piggott told the jury:

'it is for you to decide if she committed the deed deliberately and was aware of the severity of her actions at the time she did it. However if you thought that it was simply a rash act committed during a period of intense excitement brought on by drink, then you must reduce the offence to that of manslaughter. There is a reason to believe that the blow was meant for Philip Fisher and that by stabbing the man Worthington, she was mistaken in her identification, but there is no evidence to prove that this was the case.'

Annie Bishop was brought before the judge on Friday 6 December 1872 where it was said that she did not seem to fully realise the serious nature of the crime with which she had been charged. Mr Heaton Cadman for the prosecution, outlined the case. He said that previous to the attack there had been some argument between the neighbours and a scuffle or two between the other residents in the court. He then described the events of the night, and the injured man being rushed to the Infirmary. Rosina Fisher was the first witness and although she was just fifteen years of age she was described as diminutive girl who looked more like a girl of nine or ten.

She told the court about being called a foul name by the prisoner which had caused her father to interfere. She was cross examined about her uncle Charles, and said that she had seen him and Mr Bishop scuffling a few weeks earlier. Although she was asked where her uncle was when the deceased man was stabbed, she replied that she could not say rightly where he was when the incident took place. When asked the reason why, she said that none of the family had seen him since the night that he had been fighting with the neighbour. Rosina concluded her evidence by saying that when she picked up the knife, before the prisoner took it away from her, she had not seen any blood on it.

Police Constable Smelt stated that the day after the incident, he had asked Henry Bishop for the knife and was given one. However when it was shown to the previous witness, she said that it was not the same one that she had picked up on the night. The officer said that when the prisoner was taken into custody, she already had a black eye. Before the prosecution Mr Cadman rose again to speak, the defence counsel Mr Blackburn announced that he objected to this line of questioning. The judge stated that as far as he could see the whole scene had been one of confusion and scuffling, and that the jury might like to hear how Mr Cadman submitted the matter to them.

The prosecution maintained that having had the scuffle with Philip Fisher, the prisoner had time to cool off and deliberate what her next action should be. He stated that despite this:

'she deliberately and maliciously armed herself with a knife and thus acted the part of a deliberately vengeful woman'.

Mr Cadman said that if the jury saw this as her using the knife with the intention of committing grievous bodily harm, then she was guilty of murder. The defence, Mr Blackburn stated that the whole evidence for the prosecution was obscure, and the witnesses evidence statements showed them to be unsatisfactory in their recollections. He stated that 'there was so much doubt in their descriptions, that the jury might easily come to the conclusion that the prisoner had not struck the blow at all'.

The prosecution claimed that although the witness Goodison had identified the prisoner holding the knife, he had also admitted to having some alcohol that night, so he declared that his statement cannot be taken as fact. Mr Cadman said that the jury had to remember that his assertion was not corroborated by any other witness. Mr Blackburn then queried the fact that Fisher's brother Charles had been seen fighting with Mr Bishop a few weeks earlier, but he questioned 'where was Charles Fisher now, if his own family had not seen him?'

The judge Baron Piggott summed up for the jury and he emphasised the difference in law between the crimes of murder and manslaughter, before going over the evidence in great detail. He queried the fact that at first, he had thought the difference in the witnesses testimony was due to the darkness in the court, but now he thought it more because they had all been drinking. He told the jury they had three things to consider. He asked:

'Were you satisfied that the injury had been administered by the prisoner. Secondly was the act done under malicious circumstances and with the intention of doing grievous bodily harm. Thirdly did you think there was provocation of such nature as to disturb her reasoning power. If you think that the act was committed under great excitement, then you must consider it to be manslaughter.'

The jury took his words to heart and took just twenty minutes to find Annie Bishop guilty of the lesser crime of manslaughter. The judge then addressed the court and said that in the interests of society, that a lesson should be learned from people of the prisoners class who thought they could take the law into their own hands. He stated that she must therefore undergo a severe punishment and that would be penal servitude for twelve years. Annie Bishop showed no emotion as she was led down the steps, into the cells below to start her prison sentence.

Chapter Fourteen: Ann Elizabeth Guy.

On Tuesday 15 September 1874 two women were arguing at a lodging house where they were both staying on Silver Street Head, Sheffield. It was about 4.15 pm and it was one of those sordid crimes where both women were drunk and one of them died under very suspicious circumstances. By 4.30 pm the woman laying dead at the bottom of a staircase was a 45 year old known prostitute called Margaret Moore. The woman who, it was alleged had pushed her, was said to be a middle aged woman called Ann Elizabeth Guy. Inevitably the police were called to the property and Ann Guy had been arrested. She was brought before the magistrates charged with causing the death of Margaret Moore the following day.

It was a very short hearing as the Chief Constable simply asked the bench for a remand until after the inquest had taken place the following Friday, which was granted and the prisoner was then removed. The inquest into the death of Margaret Moore was held by Coroner Mr D Wightman at the Central Police Offices on Castle Green on Friday 18 September 1874. The prisoner was in attendance, in the custody of an officer from the Coroners officer. The jury were first taken to see the body which still lay in an outhouse in Silver Street Head, next to the lodging house where the woman had died.

The inquest was then opened and the first witness was the Police Surgeon, Mr Arthur Hallam who had previously worked at the Sheffield Infirmary. He told the coroner that he had undertaken the post mortem on the dead woman. He stated categorically that the death of the victim had been caused by dislocation of the neck, which had produced pressure on the spinal cord. Mr Hallam carefully described the woman's injuries, the main one of which was a contused wound about 3 inches long at the back of the head. The police surgeon had noted that the deceased woman's back was heavily bruised which, although these were not serious wounds, they would have been caused at the same time as she fell or was pushed down the steps.

He told the inquest that the subject's internal organs were diseased as one would expect in the kind of life the woman lived, although they had not contributed to her death. Mr Hallam gave his opinion that from the condition of her organs, it was obvious that the woman had been a heavy drinker. The next witness was called Mary Herrin, who was the wife of the keeper of a beer house known as the Cock and Bottle of Hawley Lane, Sheffield. She said that she had been an old acquaintance of the deceased. Mary told the jury that Moore had gone to her beer house around 4 pm and asked for a drink, but she would not serve her as she could see that she was already quite drunk.

The witness said that Ann Guy and Margaret Moore were both staying together at the lodging house on Silver Street Head and that a few weeks previously Moore had put out her shoulder whilst drunk. While the woman had been incapacitated, the prisoner had moved in with her. The coroner asked the witness if she knew if there had been any ill-feeling between the two women, to which she hesitated before replying that she did not know of any. Elizabeth Greenwood who also lived at the lodgings with her husband, told Mr Wightman that earlier on the night of the incident, she had stopped Margaret Moore entering the house, because she had a man with her. She told the court that she knew that the woman wanted to take the man inside 'for an immoral purpose' so she refused to let her in.

Much later Elizabeth said that she had been going upstairs in the dark when she felt the body of a woman lying on the bottom step. She got a candle and lit it and by its light she could see who the woman was, and it was clear that she was in a dying condition. Elizabeth told the coroner that there was a lot of blood, which had come from the woman's head on several of the steps. Other lodgers gathered around her and the witness was told of an argument earlier in the day and how it had been said that the deceased had been pushed down the stairs.

Just then Ann Guy appeared at the top of the steps and Elizabeth said to her 'see what you have done' to which the prisoner made no reply and just turned away. A doctor was called out, but it was clear that the woman was already dead. The witness gave evidence that a row had broken out between the two women on the night before the accident, when they had argued over some money. Margaret had accused Ann of spending a sixpence which had belonged to her. Even though Ann denied it, Margaret had told her 'I will have it out of you one way or the other'.

A man called John Jackson a furniture dealer who lived in the same yard as the lodging house, told the inquest that the back of his house faced that of the front part of the lodging house. He said that he had seen Ann Guy return back to the house around 4.20 pm and he could see that she was very intoxicated. Ten minutes or so later Margaret appeared accompanied by a man. Just a few minutes later a little girl belonging to another neighbour called Herrin, ran into the yard shouting that 'Maggie' was dead. The girl claimed that she had seen Ann Guy push Margaret Moore down the stairs.

After hearing what the little girl had said, Jackson said that he had gone into the house and seen that the woman was lying at the bottom of the stairs and that she was clearly dead. The witness said that both women were well known to the police and they both had bad characters. Another woman called Sarah Godby was washing at Mrs Herrin's house, the Cock and Bottle and she had also noted Margaret Moore returning home with a young man in tow. She told the inquest that the couple were very drunk and she had a pretty good idea what they were up to. Just a few minutes later Sarah saw the man leave and then heard a fearful row break out inside the house, before the sound of clattering as if someone had fallen down the stairs.

She claimed that she took little notice, as she knew that both women were very drunk. Soon after Ann Guy came into Mrs Herrin's house and told her 'I have fettled old Mag this time.' Godby told her to 'mind not to be fettled herself' before the prisoner staggered off. When the witness heard about Margaret being found at the bottom of the steps, she said that she went into the lodging house to see for herself. There she saw the woman lying with her head still on the third step up from the bottom and she too noticed that there was much blood. Also watching was Ann Guy and the witness said to her 'you have done this' but the woman denied that it was anything to do with her.

The next witness to be brought before the inquest was the eight-year old little girl belonging to Mrs Herrin. The child, whose name was Emma was not surprisingly, very nervous to be brought into the formal inquest room. She began to cry when she was asked questions. In the end all the coroner could get out of her was that the prisoner went into the house first, followed later by the deceased woman. After that, no amount of encouragement could make her speak or say anything further, so Mr Wightman sent her home to her mother. As this little witness left the inquest room, the coroner began his summing up for the jury.

He said that although he had heard testimony to say the two women were drunk and had quarrelled, no jury would convict on that evidence alone. Mr Wightman said that he had heard the little girls allegation, but unless the evidence of a child could have been supported by someone else it would not stand up in a court of law. He therefore would not advise the jury to send a person for trial unless there was a reasonable chance of a committal. The prisoner Ann Guy was then interviewed by Mr Wightman.

Under oath she told him that she was the wife of a man called Isaac Guy, but they had not lived together for eight years. The witness said that she was sharing a room with the deceased, and on Tuesday morning the deceased woman was already drunk at 11 o'clock in the morning. Ann said that she had asked the deceased woman for a return of the sixpence which she had lent her the night before. She had promised to pay her back, but now she told her that she had spent it. The witness admitted to flying into a rage, and in order to get out of her way, she had gone to Mrs Herrin's house and stayed there until 5 pm when she returned back to the lodging house.

Shortly after her return she heard Mrs Greenwood shout and went to the top of the stairs to see what was the matter. To her astonishment she saw her lodger lying at the bottom of the stairs and Mrs Greenwood was accusing her of pushing the other woman down the stairs. Ann told her that she had done nothing of the sort and hadn't even been at home since that morning. The witness was then asked by the coroner if she had told Mrs Godby that she had 'fettled' the deceased, and she agreed that she had, but it had just been said as a joke as it was a word used often by the deceased herself.

Mr Wightman then was informed that the little girl, Emma Herrin and her mother had come back into the inquest and were waiting outside the room. So he tried once again to take the little girls evidence. Kindly he suggested that she come and sit by him. This time probing her more gently, the coroner managed to elicit from her that she had been in the lodging house on that Monday afternoon. She said that shortly after the deceased woman had gone upstairs, she heard an argument breaking out. The girl said that she saw the prisoner catch hold of Margaret's dress and not push her, but rather she pulled her towards where she was standing on a lower step.

That was when 'Maggie' as she called her, overbalanced and fell. However the little girl, was still very scared of the official proceedings and it was only with the greatest difficulty that she could be made to answer any questions. The coroner finally thanked her before sending her to where her mother was waiting outside in the passage. After the girl had gone, Mr Wightman commented that her evidence would be useless at an assize court, even if she could be made to speak more clearly. He predicted that the judge and jury would inevitably decide that the witness would be too young to understand the meaning of an oath.

He also stated that there was a possibility that an accusation might be made that after being sent home, that she had been instructed in what to say by her mother. Therefore Mr Wightman advised the jury to forget her evidence all together. He re-iterated that the judge would not take the word of an eight year old child in a case of manslaughter, if it could not corroborated by an adult. The coroner told the jury that consequently there was absolutely no evidence to show how the deceased woman had fallen downstairs. She could have been pushed, or she might have simply fallen through her own intoxication.

Mr Wightman added that he did not for a moment believe the prisoners story, that she had not pushed the woman down the stairs. It was clear that she was already in the house at the time and had admitted that the two women had argued over money. Combined with her boast that she had 'fettled' the woman this time, he was convinced that she had done it. However the coroner concluded that without another witness apart from the child, there was little chance of a conviction being gained. One of the jury said that the girls statement had clearly said that she had seem the prisoner pull the deceased woman down the stairs by her dress.

The coroner agreed, but he said again that her evidence was useless without it being substantiated by someone else. After some more discussion between the jury they had to give a verdict that that Margaret Moore had been 'found dead'. Nevertheless Ann Elizabeth Guy was brought into the Sheffield Town Hall on Tuesday 22 September before the stipendiary magistrate Mr E M Welby Esq. The Chief Constable Mr Jackson told the court that the coroners jury had been held, and the verdict of 'found dead' had been passed. He felt there was little more he could add, as he could only bring the same witnesses before the magistrates, as had already given their testimony at the inquest.

The Chief Constable re-iterated that fact that the eight year old girl had been the only witness. However he then said that he had heard that another man had been in the house at the time of the crime. Mr Jackson said that the man who had said that he was a navigator on the railways, might have seen what had happened. However he had already left the town, although some of his officers were trying to trace him at the moment. The Chief Constable had to report that they had not found the man up to that point, however he said that his men would continue with their enquiries. He said that if the man could be found, the evidence against the prisoner might be strengthened.

Mr Jackson asked that for the time being the prisoner be remanded at large, and then if any more evidence came to light, she might be re-arrested and charged. The magistrate agreed to this and he remanded the prisoner at large and Ann Elizabeth Guy who was immediately set free. The unsubstantiated statement made by the little girl was insufficient to prove that Ann Elizabeth Guy had pushed Margaret Moore down the steps and killed her.

However what is not in any doubt is that some of the witnesses did not always tell the truth. Even the lodging house was referred to in some of the local newspapers as a brothel. Sadly the fact remains that a woman lost her life that evening, and that no one was held to account for it.

Chapter Fifteen: Mary Hirst.

This is a truly disturbing case of post natal depression at a time when mental health issues were barely understood. Even though the person concerned had been under treatment with a medical man, little was known about the condition and there was no medication available. Even the question of the woman's sanity was not established by professional medical men, but laid before a group of untrained members of a jury at the assizes.

Mary Hirst was aged 31 in the year of 1876 and was the wife of a miner called William Hirst. The couple lived at Burncross near Chapeltown, Sheffield. Mary had been in a depressed state following the birth of her latest child, Wilfred who in November was aged four months. It was known that Mary's family had a history of mental illness, and that her own mother had died a few years previously in the lunatic asylum at Wakefield. Consequently the neighbours had promised William that they would keep an eye on her during the day, when he was at work, but there was little else they could do.

On Thursday 9 November 1876 he had gone to work and no one suspected anything was wrong, until screams were heard coming from the house around 8 am. Then one of the older children ran to tell a neighbour who was hanging out her washing in the yard, that 'Mother was killing the baby with a knife.' The neighbour Mary Ann Womersley ran into the Hirst's house and saw Mary sat near the fire, in the act of cutting her own throat with the knife she held in her hand. To her horror the body of the little baby Wilfred lay on the floor, on its side beside her, its throat a mangled mess.

Mary Ann immediately went to the door of the house and screaming out for help, which was swiftly answered by a man who lived across the street called Samuel Redfern. He too ran into the house and wrested the knife away from the now hysterical Mary Hirst. He was immediately followed into the house by another neighbour called John Goddard. The two men then saw the body of the baby lying on the floor. Samuel Redfearn asked John Goddard to get some medical help quickly, whilst he stayed with the woman. Dr Drew of

Chapeltown arrived almost immediately, followed by Police Constable Ellerby who had also been summoned by Goddard.

Entering the property, they found one of the neighbours holding a clean towel to Mary's throat. Dr Drew saw that there was still some life in the child, so he attended to him first. He sewed up the wound in Wilfred's throat before then attending to the mother. He quickly established that her wound was not as deep or serious and concluded that she had probably been stopped from doing too much damage by the swift actions of Samuel Redfearn. The poor woman continued exhibiting her frantic state of mind as she moaned piteously, and tore at her hair and dress. When asked why she had done it, the poor woman just said 'no one cared for me'.

The child Wilfred was taken to the hospital in a cab, although there was little hope that he would make a full recovery. Meantime Mary was taken to the Grenoside workhouse and placed in the lunatic ward. Incredibly when she arrived at the workhouse, she was assessed by the workhouse medical officer to be sane enough to be brought before the magistrates the following morning. Mary Hirst was taken before the magistrates at the West Riding Court at the Sheffield Town Hall on Friday 10 November 1876. She was charged with the attempted murder of her child and her own attempted suicide.

The prisoner was brought into the courtroom in the custody of Superintendent Kershaw, who described the unfolding events before he asked for a remand of eight days for the prisoner. Surgeon Dr Drew gave evidence and he described the child's wounds which were very severe. He said that the throat had been deeply cut and the windpipe had been completely severed. The surgeon stated that little Wilfred Hirst was in imminent peril of its life and said that if he lived that he would not be out of danger three or four more weeks. The surgeon stated that he had attended as best as he could to the mother, but her wounds were merely superficial, and were basically just a few scratches. However he added ominously that in his opinion the prisoner was evidently insane.

As he uttered these words, the prisoner in the dock began to act very strangely indeed, convincing everyone of the truth of Dr Drew's remarks. Talking in what could only be described as a sing-song voice, Mary declared that she was listening to her mother who was in Heaven and was talking to her. The prisoner then claimed that she had been fighting Satan for three weeks now and had done her best to resist him, but he had cast a darkness over her. The poor woman began to ramble on about her deep affection towards little Wilfred, and how she had sung to him night and day.

She said how lonely she had been over the last few weeks, and then talked about how she had tried to care for her husband and her children. During the woman's outburst, one of the magistrates, Mr Rodgers and the police authorities in the court were discussing the best method of dealing with the prisoner. It was evident from what Superintendent Kershaw had said, that she was not in a fit state to remain in the police cells. Nevertheless she was in custody and so it didn't seem appropriate to send her to the workhouse or a lunatic asylum.

William Hirst was the next witness and he said that the had been worried about his wife ever since she had given birth to little Wilfred. He had taken her to see Dr Drew, but it had made no difference and that his wife had been worse for the past three weeks. The surgeon's only advice was to keep an eye on her which he tried very hard to do, but as he had to work the neighbours had looked out for her as best they could. Dr Drew had warned him that his wife may be suicidal and would require constant watching, but he had found it impossible to watch her all the time.

The surgeon and the magistrates discussed the matter and eventually it was decided to keep the prisoner locked up in police custody for a week, whilst some temporary accommodation be found for her at Wadsley Asylum. Accordingly the magistrate Mr Rodgers remanded Mary Hirst for a week and asked that during that time the police authorities would do their best for the poor woman. Sadly a few days later Wilfred lost his fight for life and now Mary Hirst was found guilty of wilful murder.

Even though it was patently obvious that Mary Hirst was clearly insane, nevertheless she was brought before judge Mr Justice Hawkins on Thursday 14 December at the Leeds Winter Assizes. When she was charged with the murder, Mary Hirst spoke in an incoherent and rambling manner. In answer to the charge she replied 'I do not know how I did it; I had nothing to do it with.' She said it in such a way that her insanity was obvious to everyone in the court. Nevertheless, the law as it stood at the time, left the responsibility up to the assize jury to decide the prisoner's fate.

The judge spelled it out for the jury as he told them that they had been sworn in, not to try the prisoner as to her guilt or innocence, but to try to establish whether she was in her right mind or not. Mr W N Price the medical officer of Armley Gaol, Leeds where she had been kept for a few weeks prior to attending the assizes, gave his opinion that the woman was clearly insane. He said that she was not in a state where she was capable of understanding what she had done, and was certainly not capable of defending herself in a court of law.

Because of this he had concluded that she was not accountable for her actions at the time the murder was committed. The judge therefore had no option but to direct the jury to return a verdict of insanity on the prisoner. The prisoner, Mary Hirst was then ordered to be kept in strict custody until her Majesty's pleasure became known.

His Lordship added that he hoped that by such confinement that she would be properly taken care of, however there was little chance this would happen. Even asylums of the period could do little except to establish a set routine for the patients within its walls. It was hoped that the mentally ill patient might recover better in a regimented and controlled environment, which it was thought would ease their confusion and despair.

I would like to believe that at Wadsley Asylum, Mary Hirst found the peace that she so desperately needed. Nevertheless the poor woman had been forced to take the life of an innocent baby before anything could be done for her.

Chapter Sixteen: Agnes Johnson.

As we have already seen in the case of Mary Anne Clayton (chapter five) fortune telling was widely practised in all the towns and cities of Britain, including Sheffield. It was becoming so prevalent that the local newspaper the *Sheffield Independent* dated Friday 12 November 1880, claimed 'it would reveal the gullibility of some people to those who are preyed on by the more persuasive fraudsters in society'. Headlined as 'Laughable Revelations' the case was presented as an amusing diversion, rather than the sordid crime it truly was.

The prisoner accused of the crime was a 67 year old woman called Agnes Johnson who had been brought before the magistrates the day before. She was charged, in the long winded language of the courts, in that she:

'unlawfully did use certain subtle craft, means and devices to deceive and impose upon one Margaret Devaney, that the giving of certain money to the said Agnes Johnson, otherwise Wilson, and the tying of the same in a certain way in a handkerchief, would be the means of obtaining a legacy for the said Margaret Devaney.'

Agnes told the court that she had been trading as a fortune teller from her house on Duke Street, Park, Sheffield for many years in the town.

It seems that at some point around the beginning of October the prisoner had met the woman called Margaret Devaney, who she knew slightly, at the bottom of South Street, Park. Margaret had been in the fortunate position of inheriting a sum of money from a previous lady employer, whose service she had been in for many years. But what attracted Agnes was the rumour that she was anticipating a further sum of money to be left to her in the future.

As Margaret went to walk past Agnes, she said to her that she 'had one fortune, and would soon have another'. The fortune teller promised Margaret that she would definitely get it, providing she allow her [Agnes] to 'rule your planets.' When the gullible young woman agreed, she told her that she would do it for a shilling. Margaret willingly gave Agnes her address on Hanson Street, Park, Sheffield and it was agreed that Agnes would visit her there a few days later. Upon her arrival Margaret handed her a shilling, before Agnes demanded another 1½d to send out for a glass of beer.

However instead of telling Margaret her fortune and after much prevarication, Agnes told her anxious client that she could not do it that day, as the weather had been so dull. She claimed that consequently she would have to wait 'until we have a clear day' in order to begin. Nevertheless Agnes had impressed Margaret, as she told her that she would rule her planets for her from her own home, and that good fortune would start for her if she gave her another 2s. So Margaret dutifully handed over the money and Agnes left, promising to return a week later.

On her next visit, the fortune teller told Margaret that she had been working hard on her behalf and that now she was beginning to do her some good. Theatrically Agnes got down on her knees, and swore that 'God would strike her deaf and blind if she was not doing Margaret some good and getting the money for her'. Agnes then made Margaret take an oath that she would never speak of their transactions, until she had actually brought her the fortune she expected, to which Margaret agreed. Then the woman had the temerity to demand another 18d and she was given three sixpenny pieces

When Agnes returned back to Margaret's house a few days later, the fortune teller was jubilant. She stated that she had ruled her planets again and that she had 'done some good for her'. As evidence Agnes showed her a sovereign which she said the fairies had brought her in return for the two shillings. When Margaret asked how the fairies had got the sovereign to her, Agnes claimed they 'came under the ground'. She said that she could increase the amount and asked Margaret for a silk handkerchief, promising her that her fortune would be revealed in the fullness of time.

When Margaret asked her how she knew, the old woman told her that the fairies had come to her in the night and told her so. Then she claimed they had danced before her so rapidly that they had made her quite ill. Agnes said that if Margaret had seen them too, they would have done the same to her. Margaret dutifully handed over a beautiful silk handkerchief and with great ceremony Agnes placed the sovereign in it, before directing Margaret to tie it up with seven elaborate knots, directing her carefully in the tying of the knots.

The next day Agnes came to Margaret's house again and assured her that she was continuing to 'do her good' claiming that she had been sitting up all night 'when the fairies came to her, and she could hear the sovereign rattle inside the handkerchief'. She told the gullible woman:

'You will be sure of the money, but I want one thing more. I want £2, as the more money there is laid down, the sooner you will get the fortune'.

At first Margaret baulked at giving the old woman any more money, but Agnes managed to persuade her yet again and so eventually she agreed. However she told the fortune teller that she didn't keep such large sums in the house and would need to go to the bank to draw it out. The two women went to the bank and Agnes waited outside while Margaret got the money.

As she emerged, Margaret gave the two sovereigns to the old woman, who again put them into the same silk handkerchief and took it away. A few days later she returned and again re-assured Margaret that she was doing her some good, but asked for 6d saying she had not broken her fast that morning. Margaret at first refused, but then Agnes told her if she gave her another £2 she would return all the money with interest by Thursday. Unable to resist the thought of such easy money, Margaret told her that she would have to again get the money from the bank.

Agnes told her she had some errands to run and the two women agreed to meet in Sheaf Street, Sheffield, in order for her to hand over the money. Accordingly a few minutes later they met and Margaret handed over four half sovereigns and Agnes, promised to return on the Thursday. Needless to say on the day appointed there

114

was no sign of Agnes, so Margaret went to the house where the fortune teller had told her she lived on Duke Street, Park. There she saw her son and when she asked him where his mother was, he told her that she was out of town and had been gone since the Monday.

Only at that point did Margaret finally recognised that she had been duped and had handed over the sum of £5.8s in total to the fortune teller. Angry she went to the Town Hall in order to take out a summons against Agnes Johnson. Only then did she find out that she was well known to the police authorities for her fortune telling, both as Agnes Johnson and also as Agnes Wilson. Margaret took out a summons against her and a few days later the fortune teller was found, arrested and taken into custody.

Now brought before the magistrates, Agnes was defended by Mr Fairburn, who cross examined Margaret as she gave her evidence. The defence asked Margaret Devaney if anyone had seen her giving her the money to the prisoner, to which she told him that it had been agreed in the beginning that there would be no witnesses. Margaret told Mr Fairburn this was because Agnes Johnson herself had always stipulated that no one else was to be present when she came to the house or the fortune telling would not work.

The defence asked her if she had promised to make the prisoner a handsome present when she came into the inheritance, which again Margaret denied. Police Constable Smith was the next witness and his evidence was crucial in the possible real reason why the money had been handed over to the fortune teller. He told the magistrates that he had received the warrant for the arrest of the prisoner, but could not find her in Sheffield. Then the constable said that he was given some information that Agnes Johnson was in custody in Retford and so he went there to serve the warrant.

The constable said that the Inspector of Police at Retford had read out the charge to the prisoner from the Sheffield warrant in the cell at Retford station where she was being held. However when Agnes heard the charge, she claimed that she had 'got some money from Margaret Devaney, but it was not for fortune telling, but for doctoring'. When Constable Smith was asked by Mr Fairburn if the prisoner had told him what kind of doctoring she had undertaken, the officer seemed to be slightly put out.

Plucking up courage, he said that he had realised that the matter had been somewhat delicate, when the prisoner's first question was to ask him if he was a married man, to which he replied that he was. Agnes had then admitted that Margaret had told her on the first visit to the house that 'she was in trouble'. Then the prisoner described how she had examined Margaret Delaney's body. Given the coy attitude of the newspapers of the day, it must be deduced from the missing part of the evidence that it was an intimate examination.

As the constable completed his description, Mr Fairburn lightened the mood in court by asking him 'did she offer to tell your fortune' to which there was much laughter in the court. Unabashed, the officer shook his head and said 'no sir, I did not ask her'. Throughout the hearing of the trial and the comments made by the prisoner and the defence solicitor, it was reported that there had been so much laughter in the courtroom, that the magistrates were forced to take charge. They warned the large numbers of people assembled against such frivolity in a court of law.

The chair to the magistrates said that the law took the crime of fortune telling very seriously indeed and therefore if the observers at court did not show some restraint, he would have no option but to clear the court. Then the investigation into the case resumed. Mr Fairburn stated that in his eyes there was simply no case for the prisoner to answer. He pointed out that the Act against fortune telling includes the words 'palmistry' but said that there was no evidence that the prisoner ever took hold of, or tried to read the woman's hand.

The Chief Constable interrupted at this point and referred to a part of the evidence where the prisoner 'told her lines' but the magistrates, seeing the difficulty in this, simply asked Mr Fairburn to 'pass on to another point'. Then the defence went to the phrase used by the prisoner in that 'Margaret Devaney had been in trouble' which he explained was a euphemism for being pregnant. The defence stated that he had not cross-examined the witness about it, not because he did not believe his client, but because it was such a delicate matter, that he did not like to refer to it.

He said the prisoner had told him distinctly that was why she received the money, which she claimed only amounted to 9s 6d, not the sum the witness had said she had paid her for promising her a fortune. There was some more discussion on the exact wording of the law which as the magistrates pointed out was 'pretending to tell fortunes' which is what the prisoner did. He told Mr Fairburn 'you cannot get over that'. The defence responded:

'if you really think this woman did not pretend to tell the prosecutrix's [Margaret Devaney] fortune, I cannot say any more. Her evidence is not corroborated by any other witness, and there is the fact that the prisoner told me the same story to Police Constable Smith as she told me'.

The magistrates said, but 'she was forced to tell you the same as she had told him, to which Mr Fairburn had to admit that she had. However he still maintained that the charge of fortune telling had not been quite proved.

The Mayor at this point said that there was no reason to doubt the prosecutrix evidence, and the only question remaining was what punishment to give the prisoner. He stated that as the law stood they were perfectly entitled to imprison Agnes Johnson for three months, but after more discussion the bench thought that 21 days would suffice. The prisoner was then removed from the court.

The accusation that Agnes Johnson had been possibly paid to perform an abortion on Margaret Devaney was not as outrageous as it might at first sound. The art of fortune telling was closely linked with that of abortion as can be seen in a previous book. In Chapter 21 of 'Sheffield's Dark Heart' (the second book of a 'dark' trilogy by this author) a man called Henry Simmonite advertised himself as a 'fortune teller and herbalist' who also practised this sordid, underground trade.

However if this was so, and its hard to get beyond the coyness of the newspapers reporting on the case, the sentence of 21 days imprisonment seems very light for the time. The only conclusion I can come to was that Margaret Devaney importuned Agnes Johnson for an abortion, which wasn't actually carried out. Only when through the talk of fairies, did Margaret begin to realise that she had been duped, did she then take out the summons, clouding the truth with her statements about having her fortune told.

Chapter Seventeen: Bridget O'Rourke.

On the night of 4 December 1880, a row was in progress between 59 year old Bridget O Rourke and her husband Thomas, who was aged 51. As was usual for this couple, they were arguing about money. However neither of them expected that this row was to have a much more serious ending than either could have anticipated. The discrepancies in the reported statements of this case caused great confusion to both the police and the official enquiries which followed. However the outcome was the same. At the end of that night a man was burnt about the head and shoulders leading to his death in great agony.

The couple had been married for forty years and they lived in one of the many dark courts which proliferated in Sheffield, this one being situated just off Trippet Lane. O'Rourke was a bricklayers labourer and they had a married daughter. This particular argument had started about some money which Rourke had wanted to give to their son-in-law. He had been counting out some money on a table that sat in the middle of the room. Bridget accused him of having more money which he had hidden from her. O'Rourke did not deny it, but he said something about it being hers anyway.

Suddenly, in temper Bridget picked up a paraffin lamp which had been stood on the table in between them, and in a passion of anger threw it at her husband. In seconds the lamp hit the man on the chest and his clothes burst into flames and he began to scream. The attention of the neighbours was quickly drawn to the crash and the screams they had heard from the house. Some of them entered the house and found Bridget standing there with a wild expression on her face, and flames coming from her husbands beard.

O'Rourke's hair had caught fire and his face and body were badly burned. The base of the lamp, which was estimated to weigh something like 3 lbs had hit him on his head and as a consequence blood was also pouring down his face. Flames had also engulfed the table, which was described to be rectangular and about 3 feet long and 20 inches wide. The neighbours took the poor man out into the yard and getting water from the pump in the middle of the yard, managed to extinguish the flames.

The *Sheffield Daily Telegraph* dated 11 December 1880 described the neighbours account of the gruesome scene. Its said that O'Rourke:

'Could not see anything as the hair of his head was very thick, and the paraffin had saturated it so profusely, and the fire burnt it so severely, that he screamed in agony from the excruciating pain. The house, the door and the court were besmeared with blood, and particles of the unfortunate man's burnt clothing were strewn about the ground the next day.

Neighbours also said that O'Rourke had the most difficulty in talking, as the paraffin had also entered his mouth and set fire to the inside of his mouth. Finally the neighbours managed to put out the flames and Police Constable Parkinson was brought to the house.

He took charge and the badly injured man was taken to the Sheffield Hospital and Dispensary in West Street, where he was attended to by two house surgeons called Mr Willey and Mr Pepler. They examined him and found that his burns were most extensive, and he was in a most critical position. Bridget was soon arrested and taken into the police station before being confined in a cell charged with unlawfully wounding. The surgeons had told the police that her husbands recovery was greatly in doubt and the following morning O'Rourke was reported to be still lying in an unconscious state at the Hospital.

However by Monday 6 December, Thomas O'Rourke had recovered sufficiently to make a dying deposition. As a consequence he was attended by a Justice of the Peace, Mr W E Laycock Esq., and the Chief Constable, Mr Jackson. They were met at the door of the hospital by house surgeon Mr Willey who conducted the two men towards the ward. On the way he told them that the poor fellow was so dreadfully burned, that his recovery was pretty hopeless. They arrived at the man's bedside to find the upper part of his body covered in bandages and he gave the appearance of a man who was completely exhausted.

Bridget O'Rourke was also brought into the ward in the custody of Constable Parkinson and she made as it to throw herself at her husband, but was restrained by the house surgeon. The Chief Constable explained to the injured man that they had come to take his account of what had happened on the Saturday night. Thomas O'Rourke was able to respond to questions made to him and he told Mr Jackson that he had been counting some money when the argument started. At this point the prisoner made as to interrupt her husbands statement, but she was told by Mr Laycock that she 'must be quiet'.

The man in the bed then described how she had thrown the paraffin lamp at him, which had set his clothes on fire. He said that he had the most pain when the handkerchief around his neck proved so difficult to get off as it was fire. O'Rourke explained that he had knotted it twice and could not get it over his head. When the man was asked what his wife had done when he was on fire, he said that when Bridget realised what she had done, she ran outside into the courtyard. At this point O'Rourke sounded rather exhausted and he asked for some soda water, which was given to him by a nurse.

As he recovered slightly, Mr Jackson asked him if he or his wife had been drinking that night and O'Rourke said that he had only had a gill of beer at some time that morning. Mr Jackson asked the injured man if his wife had tried to put out the fire, which he agreed that she had. He was also asked if anyone else had been in the house at the time, to which O'Rourke answered that there wasn't. At this point Bridget was asked if there was anything she wished to say to the prisoner, but she replied that she only wanted to give him Gods blessing.

Mr Jackson asked the man to confirm that he had been married to Bridget for forty years and O'Rourke confirmed it and also said that in that time they had barely argued more than half a dozen times. The badly injured man said the lamp was an old one and had no globe on it. It had only cost 3s 6d and they had it for many years.

Bridget cried out in anguish that she wished that it was her lying there and not her husband, but she was ignored by the two officials. O'Rourke was then asked to signed the deposition and the prisoner too made her mark on the document before being taken back to the cells.

On Saturday 11 December Thomas O' Rourke died and Bridget was once again brought before the magistrates, now charged with his death. Detective Superintendent Battersby asked for a remand for the prisoner until after the inquest, which was due to be held on Monday 13 December, which was agreed. The magistrates remanded the prisoner accordingly. The inquest on Thomas O'Rourke was held at the Hospital and Dispensary on West Street on Tuesday 14 December 1880 by Coroner Mr D Wightman.

Bridget O'Rourke was present and it was reported that although she appeared to be 'very down hearted and grieved' she continually nevertheless to constantly interrupt the proceedings. The first witness was the prisoner's son-in-law, a man called called Henry Lambert. He said that around 11 pm on Saturday 4 December he went to the house and asked Bridget for a shilling from some money which she was holding for her daughter. Lambert said that he had some drink, but was sober enough at the time. However Bridget had been told by her daughter, not to give any of the money to her husband and so she refused.

When Henry told her that her daughter had wanted him to get the money for herself, Bridget replied that she would give it to her daughter when she next came to the house. She told him that the money was some which his wife had asked her mother to save for him and not to give any to him. O'Rourke roughly told her to 'give it to him or I will' but Bridget still refused. When Lambert got up to go, her husband said to him 'come here Harry I'll give it thee' but the prisoner told him 'you'll do nothing of the kind.'

O'Rourke declared that he would and Henry then said that hearing his words, Bridget ignored the pair of them, but she proceeded to fill up the lamp with paraffin and to trim the wick. Henry Lambert said, after a moment or too when no more words had been spoken, he said to his father-in-law 'am I to have this shilling then Tom' and the deceased man went to give him a shilling out of his own pocket. At this point, Bridget began to interrupt the proceedings in the courtroom anxious once again to tell her side of the story. However the coroner stopped her again, telling her that he would hear her account later.

Crucially then Henry Lambert stated that in temper, Bridget had thrown the lamp hard on the table and as a result the glass broke and burning oil went all over her husband's neck and chest. It covered him in flames and the fire blazed high up above his head. The witness said he pulled his own coat off and threw it over the deceased man, but it was not large enough to extinguish all the flames. Lambert said that he then starting looking for a larger mat or something to cover the man with, to stifle the flames, however before he could do anything O'Rourke ran outside into the yard.

The coroner asked the witness if he had seen who put out the fire on the man in the yard, but when Lambert said he hadn't, Bridget interrupted again and said 'I put it out'. Ignoring her, the coroner asked him if that was true to which the witness stated that 'it might have been'. Knowing that this was the crux of the matter, Mr Wightman asked him again 'then you didn't see her put any flames out' to which the witness answered that he did not, admitting however that she might have put the flames out when the deceased man was in the yard and he was still inside the house.

Lambert said that was all he knew, but he confirmed that the couple had not been quarrelling during the half an hour that he had been in the house. He had just said that the couple had been drinking when the prisoner interrupted again and said 'No I'm sure I wasn't drinking anything.' Lambert said he had accompanied the injured man in a cab to the Hospital, along with two other young men. However when he returned back to the house on Trippet Lane, he found his mother-in-law standing in the yard 'like a wild woman'.

The witness told the court that the next morning he had gone to the Hospital and seen O'Rourke who had a sensible talk with him, and he had seemed to be quite lucid. At this point the coroner asked him to identify a table which had been placed in the inquest room. The witness said that the last time he had seen it was at the house on Trippet Lane. He was then asked to indicate the positions of the man and his wife when the incident had taken place, which he did. However crucially, when he was cross examined by the coroner, the witness could not positively swear whether the lamp was actually thrown at the man or the table.

Lambert also claimed that he did not know if the glass reservoir on the lamp which had contained the paraffin, had been cracked or not. Then the prisoner was asked if she wanted to ask the witness any questions, and it was reported that questioned him in a most violently manner. So angrily did she start to cross-examined her son-in-law that she made him break down in tears. The prejudice against Irish people was evident in the account of the *Sheffield Daily Telegraph* who reported:

'she talked most violently and the witness who was crying kept saying "that's true". However the woman's brogue and the quick way in which she poured out her words, prevented any but the witness understanding what she was saying. However the impression she gave was that he was at fault'.

The coroner merely commented that it was a great shame that the prisoner did not have any legal representation, as it was clear that she had no idea how to conduct her own defence.

The next witness to give evidence was a young man called Frederick Eaton Oliver who was a clerk in the Borough Magistrates Office. He told the inquest that he had attended at the deposition which had taken place at the deceased man's bedside at the Hospital. Oliver had been asked to write down the man's words and he produced this statement in court, which he proceeded to read out to the jury. He said that after O'Rourke had stating his name, occupation and address, the account went:

'I was in the house with her [his wife] on Saturday night last. There was a lamp burning on the table with paraffin in it. Not a deal took place. I was counting some money. My wife said I had more money.

I said "it is alright; it is all for you anyway". My wife threw the lamp at me because I did not give her the money immediately. When she threw the lamp at me, it broke. The paraffin burnt me on the face, breast and hands. My wife ran out of the house. She tried to put the flames out, but it was too late.

I saw her lift the lamp off the table when she threw it at me, but I don't know whether she used one hand or both. There was no one in the house but my wife and myself when it took place. I was brought to the Dispensary when I was burnt, and I have been here ever since. There had not been any angry words between me and my wife, except about the money. I had had a gill of ale in the morning; that was all. I was at home all the evening. It was getting on for seven o'clock when I was burnt. My wife was sober'.

Oliver stated that the statement had then signed by the witness and he had dated it, and the signatures of the witnesses were also added to the document.

Some discussion then took place about the numerous discrepancies between the deceased man's statement and that of his son-in-law. In particular was the reference to the line that 'there was no one in the place' when the witness had clearly stated that he was present. The coroner in answer to this, suggested that Lambert had given such a lucid account that they must assume that he was there and that the deceased man had forgotten due to all the trauma from the burns that he had suffered. Mr Wightman also pointed out the difference in time. The witness had said that it took place at eleven o'clock, but the deceased man said it was seven.

One of the jurors interjected that mistakes could have been made by the clerk, who perhaps mistook the words of the deceased, who was quite naturally in a very weak state when he made his deposition. The Coroner assured him that he had spoken to the JP Mr Laycock on that very matter. He had said that he had asked O'Rourke to repeat the time and had questioned whether he had he meant to say seven o'clock. The deceased man replied to both these questions in the affirmative. There was also some discrepancy in the question of whether any of the parties had been drinking or not.

Consequently the coroner had Henry Lambert recalled, who said that both himself and his father-in-law had been drinking in a nearby public house until closing time. Mr Wightman therefore told the jury that if both men were drunk, then the injuries might have confused the deceased man's remembrance of what had actually taken place. Lambert said that when they got back to the house, the only light in the room was from the fire in the grate. He clarified that the prisoner was trimming the lamp and it was lit for her by her husband from a match which he took from his waistcoat pocket.

The witness stated that when he asked for the shilling, he felt that his father-in-law dare not give it to him without his wife's consent as 'she was the master' in the house. Once again Lambert stated that he could not tell if the prisoner threw the lamp directly at her husband, or if she had threw it carelessly on the table. The coroner Mr Wightman stated to the jury that was the most important thing that the witness had said. A neighbour clarified at least one discrepancy. He gave his name as James Meekin and said he lived near door to the prisoner and the deceased man.

He said that on Saturday 4 December it was about 11.30 pm when he heard a shout. He opened the door of his own house and saw the man standing there in the yard with his body enveloped in flames, which were rising far above his head. Meekin threw a bucket of water over the man and wrapped two coats around him to extinguish the flames. The witness when questioned by one of the jury, said that he did not see the prisoner at all. Mr J M Willey the surgeon at the hospital gave his evidence and said that the deceased man had been admitted to the wards between 11 and 12 o'clock on the Saturday night.

He said that the man was suffering from severe burns of the neck, face, chest and both arms. Mr Willey described how the man had died of the effect of the burns the following Saturday. The coroner told the jury that it was now time to hear from the prisoner and for her to make her own statement. But before she did, the coroner cautioned her and reminded her that she was still under oath to speak the truth. Bridget told him that on the night of the incident, her husband had been drinking since noon. He had returned around seven, but went straight out again not returning back until 10.45 pm.

Bridget claimed that she went out leaving the lamp burning low on the table with the globe on it. When she returned however she found the globe broken and picked it up with the intention of putting it on the mantelpiece. Her husband returned and angry at what he was saying, she said that she pitched the lamp onto the table where it rolled onto the floor and broke apart. The next thing she saw were flames shooting up from the lamp which engulfed her husband's chest and arms. Bridget described how her husband had been sat with his hands leaning on his knees and the flames had shot up and covered the front part of his body.

The prisoner claimed she had followed him out to the yard and tried to put out the flames as best as she could. Bridget then concluded that she did not throw the lamp at him and it was his own fault that he got burned. One of the jury went to ask her a question, but Mr Wightman stopped him and reminded him that the prisoner had no defence solicitor present. He said that subsequently no court in England would allow her to be cross examined as it would damage her case if she said too much. He explained that he himself had tried carefully not to question her too much for this reason and that had left him in a very difficult position.

Thankfully at this point the prisoner herself stated that she had no more to say. The coroner then proceeded to sum up the evidence for the jury. Mr Wightman told them that there were three points of view that they had to take into consideration when coming to their verdict. On the one hand the deceased man had claimed that his wife had thrown the lamp at him. The prisoner had said that she hadn't. The witness Lambert had said that he did not know whether she had thrown the lamp at him and therefore the jury must make up their own minds.

The coroner said that if they thought the matter was accidental then clearly they must make that point and return a verdict accordingly. However if they thought that the prisoner had thrown the lamp intentionally or out of passion, or even dashed it against the table, they must find her guilty of manslaughter. However if they considered she had intended to kill her husband, they would have to return a verdict of wilful murder. After a very short deliberation the jury returned a verdict that Bridget O'Rourke was guilty of manslaughter and the coroner committed her to take her trial at the next Assizes on a Coroners Warrant.

Bridget was brought before the magistrates on Thursday 16 December 1880 now formally charged with 'feloniously killing and slaying Thomas O'Rourke, her husband.' Bridget was undefended, although Mr Fairburn conducted the prosecution. The bench recognising the fact asked her if she had any legal representation, but she replied. 'No your honour, I have not. The owd man was just buried yesterday and I cant afford it.' It was noted throughout that the prisoner was constantly wringing her hands and sighing loudly.

Mr Fairburn opened the case by going over the details and noting the discrepancies in the evidence from the witnesses. He then called his first witness. He was Mr Frederick Oliver who had written out the dying deposition at the man's bedside in the Infirmary. He produced the actual deposition and read out the relevant part which stated that O'Rourke's wife had thrown the lamp at him, consequent to them having an argument about money. The next witness was Henry Lambert who repeated that fact that all the three of them were drunk and he said that he had asked the prisoner several times for a shilling, but she refused.

As the witness was leaving O'Rourke had said to him 'come here Harry, I'll give it thee' and his wife said to him 'oh will you?' He said she was about to put the lamp on the mantelpiece and instead threw it and it dropped onto the table. Flames shot out from it and the deceased was soon in flames. Lambert was asked by one of the magistrates what happened to the prisoner when this happened and the witness said she had run out of the door and gone into the yard. He was asked by Mr Fairburn if she had seen that her husband was in flames and Lambert said that she had, and she looked terrified.

The chair of the magistrates [and the JP who had taken the deposition] Mr Laycock asked the witness where the deceased man had been sitting at the time and he replied that he was sat between the table and the mantelpiece. The prisoner at this point asked him 'did you see me throw the lamp at my husband?' to which Lambert replied 'no, but you threw it onto the table'. A neighbour Mary Hudson said she had heard the couple arguing that night, and O'Rourke had sounded like he was mocking his wife. She heard a crash and the deceased man ran into the yard enveloped in flames, and his wife ran up the passage into the street beyond 'like a wild woman'.

When asked if she wished to question the witness Bridget said that she didn't, giving as a reason that she was so out of her mind at the time, that she never even saw her. Further similar evidence was heard from another neighbour, before the house surgeon Mr John Willey gave his account of the man's injuries. At this point the prisoner interrupted again, crying out to the Almighty to bless her husband and saying that drink was the cause of the accident. Police Constable Parkinson told the court how he had arrested the prisoner and she had replied 'I did it. I know I did it. We were quarrelling about money. I was mad and I took up the lamp and smashed it on the table.'

Once again Bridget was asked if she wanted to say anything in her own defence and the poor woman made a rambling statement calling down blessings on her husband and saying they had lived together 'like two innocent children'. Then she stated that her husband had been very violent towards her throughout their marriage and had knocked her down about five minutes before the accident occurred. Finally she concluded that he was very drunk at the time. The bench, no doubt fed up with all the variance in the statements did not take long to give their verdict that they had found the prisoner guilty of manslaughter.

Bridget O'Rourke was brought before the Yorkshire Winter Assizes in Leeds on Friday 4 February 1881 before judge Mr Justice Manisty. Thankfully this time she was defended by Mr Vernon Blackburn. Mr Rimington Wilson outlined the case for the jury, where he now described the prisoner throwing the lamp in a 'round handed throw' spilling the paraffin which came out in a blaze setting both the table and O'Rourke alight. Henry Lambert appeared and he said that he did not believe that the prisoner meant to do her husband any harm.

He concluded 'in fact I now believe that it was quite by accident that the deceased got on fire'. He was followed on the stand by other witnesses who gave the same evidence as had been heard at the magistrates court and the inquest. Mr Blackburn the prisoners defence, then addressed the jury pointing out that there could not be a more painful case brought before them than that of the prisoners. He said that after spending 40 years in a marriage, which was now described as happy and harmonious, 'this poor woman was called upon to answer for the crime of having caused the death of her husband'.

He made the point that the deceased being under the influence of drink himself, might even have accidentally overturned the lamp himself. To which the prisoner in her grief exclaimed 'I did it, I know I did'. Mr Blackburn pointed out that any such statement made by the prisoner in a moment of deep despair could not be relied upon. The jury agreed and found Bridget O'Rourke not guilty and she was discharged.

Having researched this case carefully, I do not think that Bridget O'Rourke threw the lamp at her husband with any malice. I suggest it was done without thinking and possibly as a result of any alcohol she may or may not have taken. I don't believe that she had any evil intent towards him and it was quite plain that she was so shocked, that she was described by more than one witness as being like 'a wild woman'. Nevertheless her husband died a terrible death at her hands and she was lucky to escape, at the very least a long prison sentence.

Chapter Eighteen: Emma Nelson.

This is one of those cases which leave more questions than answers. As readers will have deduced by now, the finding of an illegitimate child's body was not an unusual event. Sadly there are many accounts of unwanted bodies of newly born children found on the streets and back alleys of Sheffield during the 19th century. However fewer were found in respectable homes of middle class families with evidence of murder by strangulation around their necks. When the mother had already died when the baby was found, there were no witnesses to give an account of themselves or to offer any explanation.

On Tuesday 5 November 1889 the body of a child was found at the house of Mr Charles Leedham an auctioneer, who had premises at the Old Toll Bar House on Langsett Road, Sheffield. The body was found in a black box by a servant girl called Lucy Mettam in the bedroom of her employers granddaughter, Emma Nelson. Mr Leedham, on being informed of the find, immediately got in touch with the police and a constable was sent to the house. He interviewed Lucy who described finding the body the box in the bedroom of Emma Nelson, who had died on 20 October 1889.

Lucy told the constable that the girl had been aged around 20 years and married, although at the time her husband William did not live with her. Lucy said that Emma Nelson had lived at her grandfathers house for the past 14 months. She had been taken ill on Friday 11 October and had taken to her bed complaining of pains in her arms and chest. The servant girl said that Emma had been attended to by surgeon Mr Waddell. He had first come to the house on Monday 14 October and diagnosed her with rheumatism and heart disease.

After her death, on Sunday 20 October, he had signed the certificate giving the reason as heart disease. Lucy said that after the girls death, her mother had arrived at the house and Mr Leedham asked herself and the mother to look through his granddaughters things for her marriage certificate.
He thought it only right that Emma's husband be informed of his wife's death. Lucy said that she had looked into the woman's clothes

box and to her horror had found the body of a fully formed female child. The two women both saw that round its neck had been a white pocket handkerchief which had obviously been used to strangle the child soon after it was born.

The coroner, Mr D Wightman had been informed and he arranged an inquest to be held at the Mortuary on Thursday 7 November 1889 and Inspector Moore was in attendance on behalf of the police authorities. Mr Arthur Hallam was the first witness and he told the inquest that he had held a post mortem on the body of the child, although it had not been easy, due to the decomposition which had taken place. He found evidence that after birth, the child had taken a breath, but he had deduced that it had only lived for just a few minutes. Mr Hallam confirmed that the handkerchief had been wound around the neck so tightly that, when he removed it, there was a red mark of constriction left. The surgeon added that would have undoubtedly restricted the child's breathing.

Internally he had found extraversion of blood under the skull, in particular over the right temple bone. The internal organs were healthy, as one would expect in a young child. However there had been a great protrusion of the tongue, from which he deduced that the child had died from strangulation. He gave his opinion that the child had been strangled soon after its birth. The next witness was a woman who had known the deceased woman for about ten years and who had been called in to nurse her in her last illness. She was called Alice Marsh and she told the coroner that Emma Nelson had been just 20 years and 23 days when she died.

Her husband was a man called William Henry Nelson and he had been a blacksmith. However she told the coroner that he was now better well known as a race runner or 'pedestrian' as they were known at that time. These were sportsmen who ran races or completed marathons for money. The witness explained that the couple had not lived together for fourteen months, although Emma had borne two other children, although only one had lived. That child now lived with Emma's mother at Owlerton, Sheffield.

Alice Marsh said that the young woman had taken ill about the 11 October and on Friday 18 October she was sent for to nurse her. The patient had complained of a pain under her arm and the surgeon Mr Waddell had asked for her to apply a poultice, which she did. On the following day Saturday 19 November the girl felt much worse and so Alice sent for the doctor to attend, and he brought another surgeon with him to the house. She overheard the two doctors talking and they said that Emma had chronic rheumatics and heart disease. Mrs Marsh stated that she had stayed with the patient overnight, but on Sunday 20 October she then went home.

The witness said that she had not been home very long before they called her back saying that the girl was failing. She had not been at the house for very long, when at 10.30 Emma Nelson died. Mrs Marsh told the inquest that Mr Leedham was still in bed when she went to inform him that his granddaughter had died. The doctor was immediately sent for and when told that his patient had died, he replied that he was not at all surprised. The witness was then asked if she had any idea that the woman she had nursed so assiduously had given birth to a child, but she said that she had no idea that she was even in the family way.

Mr Wightman asked Mrs Marsh if she thought that the baby might have been born before she attended to Emma and she agreed that it must have been. However the witness concluded her evidence by stating that as the young woman had not lived with her husband for some time, the child could not have been his. One of the jury asked Mrs Marsh if there had been any signs that the woman had given birth at all in the bedroom, but the witness said not. However she said that Emma had not got out of bed whilst she had been in the room, and she had refused to have the bed made.

The patient had also refused to let the doctor examine her properly and had just described her symptoms to him. The witness said that the deceased woman had told her that the only pain she had was in her arm. Returning back to the finding of the body the coroner asked Mrs Marsh what made her think that the child had belonged to the deceased woman. The witness said that the child must have been Emma's as it had been wrapped in some of her clothing. She described them as being a blue and white skirt, a piece of sheeting and a handkerchief tied around the neck.

Mrs Marsh stated that the skirt was Emma's as she had been informed by one of the servants and the sheeting was the same as was used in the rest of the house. She admitted that it was only the handkerchief she was unsure about. The next witness was the mother of the deceased woman, Mrs Charlotte Carreer and she said that her daughter had lived with her grandfather since she had been about three months old. Only when she was married did she leave and go to Manchester to live with her husband. However that was not for long before she returned back to Sheffield. Mrs Carreer admitted that she had not been in her father's house for ten years due to a family argument.

Therefore she was shocked when he sent for her to inform her that Emma had died. When she arrived at the house her daughter had already been washed and laid out on her bed. The coroner asked her if she had any contact with her daughter whilst she lived at her father's house. Mrs Carreer said that although she had not been inside the house, she had often seen her daughter standing at the door and they had exchanged a few words. On the day her father sent for her after his granddaughters death, he asked her to go upstairs and look in the black box that his grand daughter kept in her bedroom for the marriage certificate or any information as to her husbands whereabouts.

She and the servant Lucy Mettam went into the bedroom and found the keys to Emma's box in a pocket of one of her daughters day dresses, and that was where the child's body had been found. Lucy Mettam had picked up the bundle of clothes and had commented that the bundle was a heavy one. Mrs Carreer described how she had taken it from her and unwrapped the bundle before screaming out 'Oh its a child' when she saw what lay in among the clothing. The witness was asked about the clothing and to identify it as her daughters. But she admitted that she couldn't look at it any more, and therefore she had not seen the handkerchief around the child's neck.

The coroner asked her if she could swear that it was her daughters child, but the witness said she could not say for sure, and could only state that it had been found in her daughter box. When the nurse Mrs Marsh was re-called she was asked by a juror if she had noticed anything in the woman's body to reveal that she might have been pregnant. The witness shook her head as she replied that the girl always covered her breasts with her hands when she was applying the poultices, so she had no reason to suspect that the deceased woman had given birth to a child.

At this point Mr Wightman stated to the jury that he did not think it worth while to go any further. He told them:

'Here is a child that has clearly been murdered and the circumstances are very peculiar. I should like to see the certificate under which this woman was buried and I should like to have the evidence of Mr Waddell, the man who signed it. I don't think its possible to conclude this enquiry satisfactorily without him. There is a very strong supposition indeed – I might go so far as to say it is beyond doubt – that Emma Nelson was the mother of this child, and if she is, there is a very strong suspicion that she is the person who murdered it.

Well now she is dead, we cannot ask her in any shape or way, but if you are of the same opinion as myself, that she is the person who murdered the child, we ought to account for her in every possible way, because we cannot have her here to punish. I don't know that I ever had a more peculiar case than this is, and it is your duty, I think to bottom it to a greater extent than you can today'.

He then adjourned the inquest to the following week.

When the inquest was reconvened on Tuesday 12 November 1889 the surgeon Mr William Henry Waddell from Hillsborough was naturally the first witness. He said that when he first consulted with Emma Nelson on 17 October she complained of pains in her shoulders, her chest and her left arm. She said that she had been out in the rain and the shawl that she had been was wearing over her left shoulder had got soaking wet. Consequently it had left her with great pain in her shoulders and arms. Mr Waddell told the inquest that she had at first been attended to by another surgeon Mr Wilson. But after he had been taken ill, he sent a note to ask Mr Waddell to look at her.

The surgeon related how Mr Wilson had diagnosed muscular rheumatism in Emma Nelson and so when he examined her himself he found that she had a very high temperature. He told the inquest therefore he had given a certificate saying that death was caused in the first place by acute rheumatism and secondly from pericarditis. However the surgeon now claimed that he saw signs to make him believe that the patient had not been telling him the truth, although he did not elaborate as to what these might have been.

However the coroner asked him if he still believed that death was caused by what he had signed on the certificate. The surgeon now said that he suspected that the cause of Emma Nelson's death was caused by the birth of the child. He suggested that she might have gone out too soon after giving birth and added that she certainly was not pregnant when he saw her, but once again gave no indication what had brought him to that conclusion.

A juror asked him if he thought it possible that the deceased woman had been able to successfully remove all signs of having given birth to a baby. The surgeon told him that there was every possibility that she had, as he had certainly not seen any sign, although he admitted that she had always been in bed when he saw her. The coroner Mr Wightman then said that he wished to recall the police surgeon Mr Arthur Hallam. He asked him if he could tell how long the body of the child had been in the box, but the surgeon told him that was impossible due to the decomposition, which had slowed down due to being wrapped in clothes.

Therefore Mr Hallam judged it to be impossible to try to be more accurate. The surgeon concluded that the body might have been there for five weeks or for just one, there was no way of knowing. However, on one thing the surgeon was very clear. Asked by Mr Wightman he said that he had no doubt that the child had been strangled to death. The grandfather, Mr Charles Leedham was the next witness and he said that Emma had been married two or three years ago, but for the last fourteen months had nothing to do with her husband.

It seems that he had treated her quite badly during the marriage and so he had encouraged his granddaughter to return back to live with him. Mr Leedham stated categorically that he had never seen any sign that she had been pregnant. However he had been forced to face up to the fact that the child in the box must have been hers, as only she had full control of the box in which the body had been found. The witness said that he knew that his grand daughter had received a chill and that he remembered her coming home one day wet through. Therefore he assumed that the diagnosis given by the doctor must have been correct, and had looked for no other cause.

The elderly man stated that he could not understand how the doctors had not known that his granddaughter had been pregnant. Mr Wightman then summed up once again for the jury and the coroner admitted that this was the most peculiar case that had ever been put before him. He stated that there was no doubt that the child had been murdered, neither could there be any doubt that the child had belonged to Emma Nelson. However he thought it very peculiar that she was able to hide all signs of the birth as she had done.

Then addressing the jury he got to the crux of the matter. The coroner said:

'Could you in all conscious swear that Mrs Nelson had murdered the child. It is possible, though not probable, that someone else might have been concerned in it and might have committed the murder. They might have placed the body in the black box and put the key in the pocket of the deceased woman'

He reminded the jury that they were still under oath and must either swear that Mrs Nelson had murdered the child or leave the question open. The jury returned a verdict that the deceased had been 'wilfully murdered by being strangled by some person or persons unknown.'

This is a most curious case which I feel is not definitively answered by the evidence brought before the coroner and the jury at that time. As was usual, no enquiry was made into who the father of the child could have been. But in the claustrophobic atmosphere of most middle class Victorian homes, somebody must have known more than they were letting on. To have hidden a pregnancy was not impossible, as many of the cases in this book will show, but an illicit love affair might have been less easy to hide.

The only other female on which the suspicions of giving birth to a child might fall, was the servant Lucy Mettam of which we know nothing about. Had she been the one who had been pregnant and after her mistress had died, had taken the opportunity to hide the result of her so called shame in the black clothes box. Certainly it seems as if the coroner in his summing up for the jury certainly hinted at this possibility. She certainly would have known of the box's existence in the bedroom and no doubt had access to the key or at the very least knew where it might be hidden after the death of Emma Nelson.

Wrapping the child up in her mistresses clothes would encourage people to assume that it was Emma's baby, which had indeed happened. Had the girl feigned surprise once the body was actually found, making the comment to Emma's mother that the parcel of clothes 'was heavy' knowing very well what it contained. By handing the bundle to Emma's mother to open and discover the terrible contents, could have been a very clever move on the girls part?

Of course there is absolutely no evidence of any of this which is purely conjecture on my part, but as always I leave you to judge.

Chapter Nineteen: Sarah Brown.

Of all the evil persons in this book, the next two women are just about the worst. These were two of the most neglectful mothers to be investigated, both in in the same year by the Inspectors for the National Society for the Prevention of Cruelty to Children. In the first, the woman's own husband complained about her neglect of their child to the authorities, but then he did nothing about it and thereby allowed it to continue. Sadly despite their intervention both children would die.

The first involved a 43 year old woman called Sarah Brown, who was brought to the attention of the NSPCC on 28 January 1892. It seems that there had been a complaint which had been received by Inspector Martin in regard to the neglect of a seven month old child called Ernest Brown. The Inspector had been assigned the case, and he lost no time in securing the help of the police surgeon Dr Skinner and the two men visited the house on Hanover Street, Sheffield. There they saw a woman who was so drunk that she was holding little Ernest upside down, and had no concept of what she was doing.

Suddenly she let him go, and Dr Skinner immediately dived forward and rescued the child before it fell to the ground. Inspector Martin quickly established that she was the mother Sarah Brown, and told her that if she continued to treat her child in such a neglectful way, she would find herself in very serious trouble. Ernest was then inspected by Mr Skinner, who immediately saw that although the child was a little pale and underweight, he looked in a fairly good condition. Therefore the mother was warned that a complaint had been received, and that the Society would now be keeping a very close eye on the family.

A month later, yet another complaint was heard about little Ernest, causing Inspector Martin and Dr Skinner to again call at the house, but were unable to gain admittance even though they could hear a child crying. They visited later that evening when the father of the child, Allen Brown was at home. The little boy was examined and the two men found little Ernest to be more seriously ill, so the father was instructed to take the child immediately to the Sheffield Children's Hospital. Mr Brown wanted his son to go to some place in Derbyshire, which he said was in order to get him well away from his mother. However Mr Skinner vetoed that idea as the child was far too ill to travel.

Finally Allen Brown assented to take little Ernest to the Children's Hospital in Sheffield. The father re-iterating that he was anxious to have the child removed as far away as possible from the bad influence of its mother. Allen Brown finally took the child to the hospital as instructed. Meanwhile Inspector Martin and Dr Skinner considered ways of moving the child into a place of safety, however, for the time being they judged that the child would be safe enough at the hospital. What they had failed to anticipate however was that the next day Sarah Brown went to the hospital and removed the boy herself on Monday 29 February 1892.

The hospital surgeon had seen the child that morning, and had instructed a postcard be sent to the father telling him to collect little Ernest, together with some medicine which was needed to aid his recovery. However before the father could do anything, the little boy was already at home and still clearly still very ill, so much so that he died five days later on Friday 4 March 1892. Ernest Brown had received no special attention during the last five days of its life, as his mother Sarah continued with her neglectful parenting, leaving him with other children so that she could go to the public houses and drink.

Witnesses said later that the little boy cried a lot during his last few days at the house on Hanover Street. As one witness said 'it cried until it choked'. Despite the neighbours concerns, they saw that Sarah still went out every day. Although occasionally she might send any little girl or boy she might meet in the street, to go to the house and see to the baby. When the NSPCC heard about the death, they were no doubt filled with remorse that they had not taken action sooner to save the little boy. They informed the coroner Mr Wightman and he ordered that a post mortem be made.

The inquest was opened on Monday 7 March 1892 at the Poplar Tree Tavern on Broomhall Street on the seven month old child, Ernest Brown. In attendance at the inquest was the solicitor to the NSPCC Mr Arthur Neal as well as Inspector Martin. At the outset of the proceedings Mr Neal asked that the inquest be adjourned as the Society had not had the time to look into the case fully.

However, Mr Wightman informed him that they would just go through the preliminaries today and then adjourn the inquest to a later date.

The first witness was the father of the deceased, Allen Brown. He told the jury that he was a commercial traveller, and so he was rarely at home for any length of time. The coroner told the father that he was duty bound to warn him that 'he might not say anything unless he wanted to, but that it might possibly be used against him at a later date'. On hearing this Mr Brown declined to speak, although he agreed that he had identified the child as being his son, Ernest. His wife Sarah Brown was also was brought into the room and she too was given the same caution from Mr Wightman and she too declined to say anything apart from admitting that the child was hers.

Sarah did say that little Ernest had been seven months old and had been a delicate child from birth. The coroner stated that was as far as the inquest could go for the time being, but Mr Neal asked that the medical evidence should be heard, as that might be helpful to the case. Mr Wightman declined however, as the parents did not have a solicitor to defend them at that time. He told Mr Allen Brown that he needed to obtain some legal representation if possible when the inquest was reconvened, to which Mr Neal concurred.

The inquest was then adjourned until the following Monday 14 March at the Broomhall Tavern on Broomhall Street, Sheffield. At the reconvened inquest, Mr Brown was now represented by Mr W E Clegg. Although Sarah was present, she had no legal representative with her. Dr Pearson of Gell Street who had conducted the post mortem said that there were no external signs of injury on the child, but internally both lungs were congested, the left lungs badly so. He found that the lower half of the lung to be very congested and the upper half was bronchitic and collapsed. The bowels were pale and thin and the body anaemic and almost devoid of fat.

He concluded by saying that death had been caused primarily by congestion of the lungs, but secondarily by want of any nourishment. There had obviously been some criticism of the doctors early discharge of the child, which was illustrated by the fathers solicitor Mr Clegg. He asked the surgeon if anything would have been visible externally with the child when he had been discharged from the hospital. He admitted that externally little might be seen to have been wrong with the child, even by a trained and experienced medical man.

He added that although something might be deduced to be wrong with the child's chest, it might have been put down as just noisy breathing. On the other hand he concluded, it might easily have been overlooked altogether. Dr Pearson said that the child's weight should have been anywhere between 13 – 14lbs and yet the deceased only weighed 11lbs. Inspector John Martin was the next witness and he told the court that the father himself had drawn attention to the neglect of the child. He described being at a soup kitchen in Charles Street on 28 January 1892 when Mr Allen Brown came with a complaint about a child, whose mother left it for hours while she went out drinking.

Only when the man was more closely questioned, did he admit that he was the father of the child. The Inspector described going to the house and the door being opened by a young girl. He said that he gave her his card to the girl and asked to speak to Mrs Brown. The girl went upstairs with the card before he heard the mother Sarah shouting down 'you wont come up, you shall not see the baby.' Inspector Martin explained that a complaint had been made about the child, and therefore he was duty bound to see the child for himself. The woman then shouted down that the child's doctor was Mr Dunbar and if he wanted anything else, he had to get in touch with her husband.

Knowing that there was little more he could do without some concrete evidence, the Inspector asked the police surgeon Mr

Skinner to call the following day. Inspector Martin then spoke about a second visit he made to the house a month later on Friday 27 February, accompanied once again by Mr Skinner. Once again they found Sarah Brown to be almost drunk enough to be incapable. The Inspector said that on that occasion Mr Skinner was able to properly examine the child and that he had told the mother that the little boy seemed ill and neglected. Sarah angrily denied mistreating the child, even though she had almost dropped him, and she also denied that she had a drink problem.

Cross examined by Mr Clegg the solicitor for Allen Brown, the Inspector admitted that the father had shown evidence that he wished to do the best he could for his son. Mr William Skinner was the next witness and he told the inquest that he had visited the house in Hanover Street following a request from Inspector Martin on 30 January. The surgeon described examining the child who was in a very thin and dirty condition, nevertheless he found it to be adequately well. He warned the mother that if the situation deteriorated the NSPCC would be forced to intervene. He had discussed the matter afterwards with Inspector Martin, but the two men felt that at that time there was nothing to justify the removal of the child.

Dr Skinner related how the child had been removed to the hospital, but he admitted that he never thought that it was in such a critical condition that it might have died. Cross examined again by Mr Clegg, he said that if Ernest Brown had remained in the hospital, he had no doubt that he would have recovered. Mr Dunbar was the next witness and he told the coroner that he was the doctor who had been called in once to see Ernest Brown at the house on Hanover Street. He had been told that the child had a rupture, but Mrs Brown did not talk about anything else being wrong with him and he did not call again. The surgeon added, to no ones surprise by now, that the mother was under the influence of drink during his visit.

A neighbour called Fanny Harding told the coroner how her ten year old daughter, Nelly had been called in to look after little Ernest on several occasions while his mother went out. The witness said that she had known the family since around September of the previous year. Just before Christmas she had seen Mrs Brown drunk on the sofa and the baby was in its cradle at the side of her. Two of the feeding bottles were in the room and they were smelly and had sour milk in them, and so the witness said that she had washed them out. Since then Mrs Harding had often gone to the house and washed out the bottles for her neighbour.

On the last occasion she had told Mrs Brown that little Ernest was looking ill and he should be in the hospital, although she suspected that the mother would do nothing about it. Then Mrs Harding gave the most damning evidence which shocked the people at the inquest. She said that on 22 February she saw Mrs Brown and another woman coming into Charlotte Lane leading to the house. The two women were obviously very tipsy and Mrs Brown told her that she had been out all day.
When Mrs Harding asked her where the baby was, the drunken woman replied that she expected the child was at home. Then Sarah Brown said she 'hoped it would be dead when they got home'.

The witness continued giving her evidence to a shocked inquest as she related that on 2 March the woman had come to her house after leaving the child in its cradle at home. It was only 8 am but the woman was already drunk, and Mrs Harding could not help but notice that by noon she was exceedingly drunk. On the 5 March she said that Sarah Brown went to her house and said that the child was dead, and the witness told her 'well you have got your wish now'.

The next witness was Nelly Harding the daughter of the last witness. She said that since September, she had often nursed the baby for Mrs Brown. The little girl stated that she had often gone to the house after school, and on many occasions had found little Ernest was alone in the house and crying. Nelly described finding him cold and wet several times when, as more often than not, there was no fire in the grate. On one occasion, this little ten year old child had lit the fire herself in order to keep Ernest warm. Nelly said that the milk for the baby was often sour, and she had been forced to fetch some fresh from the shop across the road.

The young witness stated that the mother was rarely at home when she called, but would usually arrive home about 9 pm in a drunken condition. Often she had seen the mother pick up little Ernest and had often let him drop without realising what she was doing. Nelly told the inquest that she had heard Mrs Brown say several times that she wished the boy was dead. Another acquaintance of Mrs Brown was a woman called Mrs Hayter, who stated that she had known the family for some years. On 29 February Mrs Brown told her that her husband had taken the baby into hospital and she wanted it back.

The witness said that she tried to persuaded her to come with her to the Children's Hospital to see if the baby was there, and when they arrived at the ward the nurse said it was well enough to go home. Mrs Brown got a cab and the two women and the baby returned back to the house on Hanover Street. The witness claimed that at the time her friend was sober, but when she went to see how the baby was a bit later that night, she was drunk again. Mrs Hayter said that the little boy was terribly neglected and she had warned her friend that she would be in serious trouble if the authorities found out.

Mr Clegg cross examined her and she told him that the couple had two more older children, and that Mr Brown had taken them away to stay with some relatives in Birmingham. When the solicitor asked the reason why, the witness told him it was because his wife was addicted to drink and she had neglected them. Another young witness then gave evidence and introduced herself as Lily Bradley aged 12 who lived with her parents in Trafalgar Street, Sheffield. On Shrove Tuesday she said that she had seen Mrs Brown in a house on Trafalgar Street around noon, and she had asked her to go to her house and look after the baby and mend the fire.

Lily said that the woman was not sober, but she had told her that she would soon follow and would be at the house shortly. Lily said that she asked her friend Rebecca Roddis to come with her, and the two girls went to the house and found the door unlocked. The baby was almost choked from crying and in the fire place were just three tiny red pieces of coke, which gave off no heat at all. The young witness said that she picked up the baby who was cold and wet, and made up the fire whilst her friend gave the baby a bottle of milk. Lily said that he devoured it hungrily.

The witness said that by 5.30 pm there was no sign of the baby's mother and so she wrapped the baby up in her shawl and went looking for her at the house on Trafalgar Street, but she could not find her. Nelly said that she then decided to take the baby home with her. However when it got to 7.30 pm and she had to go to bed, Lily was forced to take the baby back to the empty house. There she gently lay the, now sleeping baby back in its cradle, and wrapped it up as warm as she could. Then she had no option but to leave it there on its own.

After hearing all this most disturbing evidence, the solicitor for the NSPCC Mr Neal told the coroner that he had more witnesses, but their statements were all saying the same thing. However if the coroner or the jury wanted to hear more evidence, he could bring them into the inquest room. The coroner declined and then he asked that the father of the child gave his testimony. Allen Brown took the oath and told the jury that he had been trying for some time to get his son into some kind of institution and away from its mother. He said that he had therefore been quite relieved after speaking to Mr Skinner and the child had been removed to the hospital.

The witness said that his job as a commercial traveller kept him from home for long periods, but he admitted that even when he was back in Sheffield, he stayed away from the house on Hanover Street. When asked the reason why, he told them that it was because of his wife's drinking habits. Allen Brown said that he had always paid her enough maintenance to keep on the house, but she spent it all in drink. He explained that five children had been born to them throughout their marriage, but two children had died and his other two sons were at a school in Birmingham.

Asked a question by Mr Neal, the man stated that he knew that his youngest son was being neglected and that was why he was looking out for another place for him. Between January 28 and February 28 he had been advertising for new lodgings for the mother and the child and hoped to find some where little Ernest could be properly looked after as well as his mother. Mr Neal asked him if he took any other steps to secure the welfare of the child, to which he was forced to admit that he had not. The witness then said he did not remember being reminded by Inspector Martin of his own responsibility to his son.

Cross examined, Allen Brown was forced to admit that after the baby had been taken from the hospital, he took no steps to find it another home or even another female to care for him. Brown admitted that he had not bought any medicine for the child, even though he took money to the house for his wife every week. He was reported as having said to Police Constable Wall after his son's death that 'I am thankful it has gone; it has been an obstacle to me; it has upset my plans' which he now denied saying any such thing. At this point several members of the jury asked similar kinds of questions, but Brown maintained he had always done his best for the child.

The coroner then asked the mother Sarah Brown if she had anything to add at this point, but the woman refused to make any statement. The coroner summed up the case and told the jury they had to decide for themselves if the child, Ernest Brown had been criminally neglected. If they decided that it had, then they had to decide by whom. If they found it was the mother, then it would be their duty to commit Sarah Brown for trial for manslaughter. He added ominously that they had to bear in mind that another person also had responsibility for the child, which was its father.

Mr Wightman said that it was no good the witness saying that he gave his wife sufficient money for food, if he did not see to it that his son got enough food to survive. After consulting together for about an hour the jury were almost unanimous in finding Mrs Sarah Brown guilty of the manslaughter of her seven month old son Ernest. However they added that:

'we consider Allen Brown to be also highly censurable for his neglect to the deceased, for while he knew that his wife was not attending to it, he failed to provide better care and protection himself.'

The coroner also spoke to Allen Brown and told him that he totally agreed with the jury's decision and that he was satisfied that he was getting out of this matter 'too easily and leniently'. Addressing the neglectful father Mr Wightman said:

'You have admitted you knew how your wife was behaving to the child as early as 28 January and you say you may have known of this conduct for some months before. Nevertheless you go away, and although it is true you cannot always be at home, yet with the knowledge you had, you should have seen it your duty to have take much better and many more steps than you did, for the protection of your own child. Instead of this you leave it in the hands of one, by whom you knew it was neither protected or properly treated.

The jury have drawn a distinction between you and your wife, chiefly on account of your business. Being a commercial traveller, it was necessary you should be much away from home, but if you had been in business in Sheffield and had been at home night after night, the jury would have taken a very different view of your conduct. You knew the child was being ill treated and neglected and by doing nothing, you connived at that ill treatment and neglect. That is the opinion of the jury and I can only say my opinion coincides with it'.

Sarah Brown was brought before the Sheffield Stipendiary Magistrates on Tuesday 22 March 1892. She was charged firstly with manslaughter and a second charge of neglecting the child in such a way as to cause it unnecessary suffering. As the case opened the stipendiary magistrate Mr R M Welby said that there was a matter to be cleared up before the case could be heard. He questioned whether the charge of manslaughter was an apt one to send to the assizes. Mr Clegg for the defence said that his client should only be tried on the lesser charge of neglect, as there was no evidence to support the charge of manslaughter. However Mr Neal felt that the prisoner should be charged, not just with manslaughter, but on on both counts.

Thankfully by this time she had the same solicitor as her husband had used, Mr Clegg who was now defending her. As before Mr Neal from the NSPCC conducted the prosecution. He then went through the evidence which had been brought before the coroner and the same witnesses made their statements. The magistrate Mr Welby stated that the child, Ernest appeared to have been naturally weak from birth, although he said for that alone he should have received extra attention from its mother. However she seemed to have given way to drink and therefore had neglected her duty towards her child.

Mr Clegg agreed with regard to the neglect, but again stated that the charge of manslaughter was unsubstantiated by the evidence and therefore it should be withdrawn. Mr Welby consulted with some of his colleagues, before announcing that he had come to a decision on the subject. He stated that he thought that the case as it was, should go for trial at the assizes. That would allow the judge and the Grand Jury, who were more qualified than he was to make that distinction.

Sarah Brown was brought before the judge Mr Justice Wright at the West Riding Assizes held at Leeds Town Hall on Tuesday 29 March 1892. As was usual the judge discussed the up coming cases with the Grand Jury before the trial started where it was agreed, as Mr Clegg had thought, that there was no true bill found against Sarah Brown on the charge of manslaughter and she was discharged. It appears from the reporting of the trial, that no enquiry was made into the second charge of which she had clearly been guilty. It is a sad fact that both parents of little Ernest Brown had contributed to his death and yet they had walked away Scot-free.

Chapter Twenty: Rose Bell.

The second Sheffield case was heard just a few months later, when the NSPCC learned that information had come from a workhouse official that a child might have been starved to death. The saddest part of this account was that through all the reporting, the poor little girl was not even given a name. The child's mother was a thirty one year old woman called Rose Bell, who had come to live in a house in a court off Pond Street, Sheffield with her two children at the beginning of August 1892. The house itself was a typical of the period, set in a yard with houses all around and a pump in the middle.

Rose Bell was not the usual kind of woman that the NSPCC normally dealt with. For a start there didn't seem to be any sign of poverty, as she seemed to have enough money to engage a cleaner. She had asked one of her neighbours, a woman called Mrs Hannah Holmes to come to the house and clean for her on a regular basis soon after she moved in. Nevertheless Hannah could not help noticing how thin, the youngest unnamed little girl of just a few weeks old seemed to be. Bell also had another child with her who was around two years of age, and she told Hannah that her husband had gone to America some twelve months previously.

Other neighbours in the yard spoke about how Bell often seemed to leave the children in bed together when she went out in an evening. She would usually return about 8 pm in order to pop into the house and see that the children were alright before going out again. It did not take them long to concluded that Rose Bell went out at night 'for no respectable purpose'. This probably also accounted for the fact that she always seemed to have money. It seems that prior to coming to Pond Street, Bell had taken lodgings at another house in Little Pond Street with the children. Whilst there she also regularly left the baby locked in the bedroom alone during the day, when she went out with the older child.

Her routine was usually to return later at night, put the older child to bed and then leave them both to go out yet again. Hannah Holmes had felt sorry for the little girl and asked Bell if she would let her look after her during the woman's absences, but Bell declined the offer. However on Saturday morning 6 August 1892 she did asked Hannah to take care of the child overnight the following day, while she went to visit her mother in Rotherham. Hannah agreed and that was when she noticed how thin the little girl was, as she was bathing it.

When Bell did not return the following Tuesday 9 August as promised. Hannah took the child to see Dr Skinner and explained the circumstances and that she thought the little girl had been abandoned. Mr Skinner, alarmed at the condition of the child, got in touch with the Fir Vale workhouse authorities and she was taken in. Upon admittance it was noted how thin the little girl was, and consequently she was taken straight to the children's ward. What Hannah did not know was that Bell had gone to Rotherham, not to see her mother, but because she was expecting to be brought before the Rotherham magistrates charged with theft.

When she returned later on that same Tuesday evening, Hannah told Bell that she had been forced to take the child to the workhouse. She was horrified when her neighbour told her 'well if its there, it might as well stop there'. What neither of the woman knew, was that the little girl had died at the workhouse on the Wednesday, and so it was something of a shock for Rose Bell when the following day she was told of the child's death and was arrested on the charge of cruelty to it. The Deputy Coroner, Mr B Bagshawe had been informed and had arranged an inquest to be held at the Fir Vale workhouse on Saturday 13 August 1892.

The inquest was opened by the coroner and also in attendance were the solicitor, Mr A Neal and Inspector Martin from the NSPCC. Several witnesses gave shocking evidence that the little girl had been neglected so cruelly, that she was nothing but a living skeleton. Bell was also at the inquest and when questioned said that the child had been sickly from birth and wouldnt always take the food she gave it. She also claimed that the little girl was always so small because she had been born several weeks premature, and was difficult to feed.

The first witness was the assistant Medical Officer for Fir Vale workhouse, Mr John Lewis Owen. He stated that the child had been brought to the workhouse on the evening of Tuesday 9 August. He told the coroner that the baby was in such a weak condition that she had died the following day.

Mr Owen stated that since the child's death he had had completed the post mortem, and found that externally there were no bruises or any signs of violence on the little body. However the child was vastly underweight as she was 21 inches long, but had only weighed 4½ lbs in weight. Externally the skin was wrinkled and loose, and the ribs were very prominent.

Mr Neal asked the medical officer how much a child of eight weeks should weigh and Mr Owen it should have weighed around 8 lbs. However he disproved the words of Rose Bell when he said that he saw absolutely no evidence that the child had been unable to eat food properly or that it had been prematurely born. The medical officer said that internally he found that there was a complete absence of fat on the body and the stomach held only a small amount of milk. Therefore he had no option but to give his opinion that death had been caused by starvation.

The Deputy Coroner asked Mr Owen if he had come across cases where children fed on artificial food, rather than breast milk might die of starvation, due to their body being unable to process such food. The medical officer stated that he was well aware of that, but the post mortem showed no evidence that the child had been unable to process any food given to it. The next witness was the neighbour Hannah Holmes who told the coroner that the previous Sunday she had seen the child undressed for the first time, and was shocked to notice how emaciated the little girl seemed. She told the inquest that she looked like a 'living skeleton'.

A relieving officer with the wonderful name of Lancelot Arthur Morley was the next witness and he told the inquest how the witness Hannah Holmes and Rose Bell had gone to the Vestry Office on Westbar the previous Friday to ask for a burial order for the deceased child. When the witness asked for the whereabouts of the mother, Hannah Holmes stated that the mother had deserted the child. At that point when the relieving officer went to make enquiries, Rose Bell went out and did not return. Accordingly the burial order was given to Hannah Holmes.

Another witness was Mary Ellen Thompson who ran a lodging house on Little Pond Street where Bell had lived before moving to her present premises. She told the coroner that at first when Bell took the rooms she only had the one child. It was not until the end of the first week that they saw that she had a baby, as well as the two year old. Mrs Thompson told the coroner that Rose Bell was such an unnatural mother that she would leave the children for hours at a time. On one occasion the witness said Bell went out at 9 pm and did not return until 3 am the next morning and the children were left on their own all that time.

The witness said that her father who also lodged with her, was so incensed that he told Bell that unless she treated her children better, he would send for a police officer. Eventually he suspected that the woman had a bad character [she was a prostitute] and gave her notice to leave. At this point the inquest was adjourned to the following Friday in the hope that Rose Bell would have been found and taken into custody. The coroner told the inquest that given the nature of the evidence, it would be better if the mother might be present.

On Friday 19 August 1892 the inquest was re-convened once again at the Fir Vale Workhouse and Mr Neal and Inspector Martin of the NSPCC were again in attendance. Mr Bagshawe told the court that although a warrant had been issued for the mother's arrest, she still had not been found. A widow called Elizabeth Russell gave evidence that Rose Bell had been living at Sylvester Gardens, Sheffield when she had given birth to the deceased child in June. She told the inquest that the child had been born and was fully developed and healthy. For several days after the birth she had attended to the mother as a midwife.

Mrs Russell told the inquest that as far as she was aware, Bell had breast fed the child properly, up to her leaving the house several weeks previously. However another witness gave much more conflicting evidence. Priscilla Shore told the inquest that she was a married woman and an acquaintance of Bell's and had also been present at the child's birth. She then told the horrified court that she believed the mother had given the child nothing but a dose of caster oil every morning and night.

Horrified Priscilla Shore had obtained an order for six pints of milk for the baby, from a charity connected with St Simon's Church in Sheffield, but the witness said that most of it was given to the older child by her mother. The witness claimed that she had often complained to Bell about the way in which she had neglected the little girl. The witness said that on Saturday night 9 July during the mothers absence, she had taken the child to Mr Skinner who was the honorary secretary to the Sheffield branch of the NSPCC. Priscilla told the court that she was unable to see him as he was not at home and she had been told to return back on Monday.

She had asked if there was anyone else who could see the child, but was told that there wasn't. The witness said that she had often complained to Rose Bell about the way she treated the child, but the mother just answered that she 'wished she was dead and out of her way'. Priscilla put forward her opinion that the way in which the child had existed was 'simply a system of slow murder'. She also gave evidence of Bell going out and leaving the baby locked in the bedroom at night, with no one in charge. The same surgeon who the witness had tried to see, Mr William Skinner was the next witness.

He said the little girl had finally been brought to him at his house on 9 August. He immediately saw that it was extremely emaciated and in a dying condition. He advised her removal to the Fir Vale Workhouse immediately. He had also been present when Mr Owen made the post mortem and he too believed the cause of death to be starvation, arising from prolonged neglect. He agreed with Mr Neal when he said that castor oil administered in such quantities would be highly injurious to a child of the age of the deceased.

After hearing all the evidence the Coroner summed up for the jury and he told them:

'Assuming that you are disposed to accept the theory that the child had been intentionally starved to death, it is your duty to bring in a verdict of manslaughter against Rose Bell, as she was the only person who could be held responsible. The evidence of the strongest possible kind is that the mother was in the habit of leaving the child alone in the house for long periods, and it showed that the child had practically no food for a considerable portion of its existence'

He also reminded them that every effort had been made to find the mother who had left Sheffield in such a hurry. He said that the police had managed to trace her to two or three other towns, but she had managed to escape their grasp and had not been found up to that point. The jury consulted for just a few minutes, before returning a verdict of 'manslaughter against Rose Bell.

The following day Detective Sergeant Roper of the Sheffield Police had information that Rose was staying at a house in Shaftesbury Square at Rotherham, where it seems that she had been for the last few days. He went to Rotherham immediately with Police Constable Weatherhogg and they started to make enquiries in the Square. Unknown to them, Rose had seen them and run out of the back door of the house and hid in a nearby barber's shop. Nevertheless it was not before the two officers found her and she was arrested and taken into custody at Rotherham Police Station.

As she was being marched through the town, news was heard of her cruelty to her baby and by the time they arrived at the Police Station, a large crowd were following the two officers. They were shouting insults and curses at the prisoner as she was taken into custody. Later in the day Rose Bell was handed over to Police Constable Baker of the Sheffield Police and she was removed back to Sheffield.

On Monday 22 August 1892 Rose Bell was brought before the Sheffield magistrates. Mr Albert Howe of the NSPCC, who was standing in for Mr Neal, outlined the case before asking for a remand until Saturday when he said that Mr Neal would be in attendance. Consequently on Saturday 27 August Rose Bell was brought back into court and the witnesses testimony was taken.

Police Constable Shaw described an earlier occasion when they had followed the prisoner home due to her drunken condition.

He stated that on 29 July at an early hour in the morning, he was on duty in Sheffield when himself and another constable saw the prisoner staggering along. It was plain that the woman was under the influence of alcohol, so the two officers escorted her home. Entering the house, they found the deceased and an older child alone. The younger child was found face down in the bed and in great danger of suffocation. One of the constables called Bell 'an inhuman brute' and Rose Bell replied that she 'wished both children were dead, as she had nothing to keep them on'. After hearing all the statements, the magistrates found the prisoner guilty and she was ordered to take her trial at the next assizes.

The subject of bail for the prisoner was brought up and Rose Bell said that she had friends in Barnsley who would pay the bail costs for her. However as Mr Howe pointed out, there was a great risk that the prisoner would abscond yet again and he advised against it. After much discussion it was decided that the prisoner was to be remanded in custody to give her friends chance to offer bail. Rose Bell was brought before the judge Mr Justice Wright at the Yorkshire Autumn Assizes at Leeds on Saturday 10 December 1892 charged with the manslaughter of her seven week old daughter.

She was charged with having 'wilfully ill treated, neglected and abandoned such child, causing it unnecessary suffering and injury to its health'. The prosecution was Mr Waugh and the prisoner was undefended. The prosecution outlined the case for the Grand Jury saying that the medical gentlemen had concluded:

'that starvation and starvation alone was the cause of death. The evidence pointed to the systematic neglect of this child from the moment of its birth by the prisoner, its mother. She refused to suckle the child and although on six occasions a woman called Priscilla Shaw obtained pints of milk from a charitable society for the child, the prisoner gave it to another child in every instance'

Mr Waugh said that the prisoner Rose Bell didn't seem to understand the meaning of the term manslaughter, with which she had been charged. When she was arrested she told the magistrate 'I did not beat the child: I did not poison it: and therefore how could I kill it? Mr Waugh said that the prisoner seemed to be entirely lacking of any sense of responsibility towards any of her children. However the woman was not without means to be able to provide adequate food for her children. She had even offered to pay the constable who arrested her, a sovereign to let her go.

Mrs Hannah Holmes the neighbour was the first witness for the prosecution and she described the condition of the baby when it had been left with her. She too said that the prisoner always seemed to have money, and when she left the little girl with her overnight when she went to Rotherham she had given her 2s 6d for food. Nurse Wilks the nurse at the Sheffield Workhouse stated that she remained in constant attendance on the baby during its stay in the wards. Despite she did all she could for it, the girl died the following day.

The judge said that this was a very sad case, and the question for the jury was 'had the mother wilfully neglected the child'. Mr Justice Wright however said that he was not quite sure that the whole of the evidence which the witnesses had given against the prisoner could be relied upon. He also felt that they had not got to the truth of the motive of the witnesses in making these statements. However there was no getting away from the fact that a child had been wilfully neglected until it died.

The jury found her guilty and then Mr Justice Wright addressed Rose Bell. He told her:

'The jury have properly found you guilty. The offence is a serious one for with such neglect and ill treatment, you must have known that the child would either die or probably be injured for life.'

He then told Rose Bell that she was to be committed to prison for six months.

These two cases illustrate the way in which young children could be so neglected that they died at the hands of their own mothers. Thankfully the NSPCC increasingly began to bring these cases to the public attention and the numbers gradually declined.

Chapter Twenty One: Lily Sneath.

This case is yet another of those tragic concealment of birth cases which were all too prominent in Victorian society. However by this time coroners, magistrates and judges were looking on such cases with more sympathy than previously. In this case a young girl, almost driven out of her mind with the way in which she had to hide the fact that she was pregnant and unmarried, gave little thought to the consequences of her actions. As a result her efforts of trying to dispose of the little body, not only resulted in it being found almost immediately, but what's more the finger of suspicion being pointed firmly at her.

On the morning of Wednesday 20 July 1892 a man employed as a groom called James Evans was about his duties at the house of his employer on Tapton House Road, Broomhill, Sheffield. As he went into the yard he saw a bundle of what he thought were rags in the ash pit. Evans went to investigate and to his horror he uncovered the body of a newly born, female child. Evans went back into the house and told the cook and another servant who was present called Ida Green. They both went out to examine the body before they notified the police. There had been much suspicion that the possible mother was a person had also been employed at the house as a domestic servant over the last five months.

She was a 21 year old girl called Lily Sneath whose parents lived at Brightside. The girl had put on considerable weight whilst she had been employed at the house, but when challenged had always denied that she was pregnant. A constable was sent to the house on Tapton House Road and the body of the child was removed. The employers wife spoke to the young domestic servant and soon afterwards Lily's mother arrived in a cab and took her daughter home with her. It seems that the previous night, Lily had written a letter to her mother asking for her to come and take her back to the family home.

Meanwhile the body of the little girl had been taken to the Sheffield Mortuary and the Coroner, Mr D Wightman had been informed. He requested that surgeon Dr Joseph Pearson of Glossop Road, Sheffield undertake the post mortem the following day and to report his finding at an inquest which had been arranged for Saturday 22 July 1892. Firstly Dr Pearson went to see Lily at her parents house along with Police Constable Ward. He asked her several times if the child was hers, which she continued to deny. Frustrated that he was getting nowhere Dr Pearson called her mother into the room and said that he wanted to physically examine the girl.

Only at this point did Lily break down and confess that the baby was hers. Sobbing she described how she had fainted when she was born. When she recovered she said that the little girl was not breathing, and in a panic she wrapped it in some newspapers and hid it under the bed. She admitted later placing the child's body in rags and placing it in the ash pit. Lily was then cautioned by Constable Ward and taken into custody. At the inquest a jury was empanelled and they were taken into the mortuary to see the body of the little girl for themselves.

They then returned back to the inquest room where evidence was taken by Mr Wightman. He stated that at this preliminary inquest and without the attendance of the mother, the only evidence taken would be that of identification. The groom, James Evans described finding the body and his horror when he found it was a baby. At that point Mr Wightman stated that as police were still undertaking enquiries, he he would now adjourn the inquest to Friday 19 August 1892. When the inquest was re-convened, Lily was now able to attend, and was escorted into the room by a female wardress.

She was reported as still looking pale and shaky, and was given a chair to sit in whilst listening to the evidence against her. The first witness was Dr Joseph Pearson who told the inquest that following the coroners request, he had undertaken the post mortem on the body of the little girl.

He said that externally he found that the body was that of a fully developed female child. There were no signs of injury to the body, and he put forward the suggestion that the cause of death was the lack of professional attention at the birth. As a secondary cause he stated that it might have been loss of blood from the umbilical cord which had been inexpertly cut with a pair of scissors. He stated that the child had lived for a few moments, but there was no evidence as to whether she had breathed or not after birth.

He concluded that he believed that the little girl had been born alive, but had died shortly after the umbilical cord had been severed. After the surgeons statement, Lily was asked if she wanted to say anything. When she said that she did, she was cautioned by the coroner who told her that her evidence would be taken down and could be used against her. The witness finally stated that the baby was her own and she had been born just after midnight. Lily explained that she could barely remember the details as she had fainted soon after it had been born, and when she recovered, the child was already dead.

 Lily admitted not knowing what to do, and being in a daze as she had placed the body in some newspapers and put it under the bed. After this ordeal, she awoke again at her usual time of 5 am to find she was very confused, and she took the body downstairs barely knowing what she was going to do with it. As she entered the kitchen which was thankfully empty, she wrapped the body in some rags and took it outside to the ash pit. Lily was crying as she told the inquest that ever since that morning, she had been tormented at what had happened. The girl said that she would give anything to have the baby back.

It was reported that the scene was so tragic that the people in the inquest room were equally distressed, and that included the coroner himself. In his address to the jury, Mr Wightman told them that the case 'was a miserable one'. He said that there was little point in sending the girl for trial on a charge of manslaughter, as he believed that no conviction would be obtained in any court of law on the evidence before them. He explained his predicament to the jury as he said:

'The mother, of course was liable to be prosecuted for concealment of birth, but he did not think there was sufficient concealment to justify a conviction. That however is for you to decided'.

The jury was out of the room for just twenty minutes, before they returned and stated that the child had more than likely died from the lack of attention at birth. Therefore they recorded an open verdict in case the police or magistrates might take any further proceedings they thought advisable. They were right to do so. On Wednesday 24 August 1892 Lily Sneath was brought before the bench at the Sheffield Court House. Dr Joseph Pearson once again gave information about the post mortem and his findings that the cause of death had been lack of medical attention at birth.

Ida Green the fellow servant at the house in Broomhill and the groom James Evans also gave their evidence on finding the body. Police Constable Ward described going to see Lily at her parents house and said how she had at first denied the baby was hers, before finally admitting to Dr Pearson that it was. When the girl admitted this, she told him that she was not right in her head at the time. The magistrate asked the prisoner if she had anything to say in her own defence, and Lily told the bench 'I was not conscious of what I did. I was too frightened to tell anyone.' After a short consultation between the members of the bench, Lily Sneath was then committed to take her trial at the assizes and bail was allowed.

On Tuesday 6 December 1892 when the discussions about the cases to be heard by the judge and the Grand Jury were listed before the assizes started, Lily Sneath's case was looked into. The judge Mr Justice Charles stated that he had looked over the depositions which had been taken at the coroners and magistrates courts. He had found clear evidence that the girl was not even conscious when the child died, and therefore he directed that the Grand Jury ignored the bill against the prisoner. Lily Sneath was released and no doubt returned back to Sheffield a thankful and more wiser young girl.

Chapter Twenty Two: Sheffield Prostitutes.

However the one type of women who was nominated as truly evil by Sheffield's respectable society were the women who worked as prostitutes. As was usual in such a patriarchal society, the men who went with such women were judged to be blameless, and simply too weak to resist the women's powerful thrall. Drives and missions to rid Sheffield of these 'menaces to male purity' were regularly held throughout the nineteenth century, although they were mainly unsuccessful. Women who were charged with the act of soliciting or prostitution, were brought before the magistrates where they were usually fined or imprisoned for up to a month.

Condemnation of such women of Sheffield started as early as 5 February 1820 when a letter to the Editor of the *Sheffield Independent* appeared. The writer describes the 'vice which infects many of its young inhabitants, who run head long to their own destruction.' Too ashamed to add his name the writer signed himself simply as 'A FRIEND TO MORALITY'. He claimed that the town of Sheffield had been described as 'one of the worst places that visitors have seen for this certain vice.' The letter claimed that:

'You cannot walk along the streets by night without being attacked and insulted by women, who are a very scandal to their own sex. Indeed Sir, not only women, but may I say even children (for many appear not to be above thirteen or fourteen years old) are devoted to one of the worst vices, that of female prostitution.'

Despite the fact that many people truly believed that women choosing the live of prostitution was based on her own licentiousness and idleness, could not be further from the truth. The life of a woman prostitute and the dire conditions in which she was forced to live was heard in another letter addressed to the editor of the *Sheffield and Rotherham Independent* of November 5 1837 entitled 'Fearful Facts'. The unnamed correspondent admits that he is a doctor, and as a consequence he states that his livelihood took him to some of the worst places in Sheffield.

He estimated that in certain parts of the town, he had witnessed some of the most 'abandoned women' of which he claimed there were around 2,000 at that time. The writer admitted that it was impossible to state with any certainty, but that he had spoken to several watchmen of the town and they had arrived at that estimated figure. He calculated in his letter, that if each of these women went with ten men and those men had families, then 'the vicious influence of these 2,000 harlots would affect hundreds, if not thousands of lives'.

Yet he bemoaned there was no reformers for such a class, as 'many of them have never heard a sermon and only enter a church on their way to the grave'. He stated that he had:

'Always found these women drunken, dirty and diseased. They mostly finish the nights crime by getting drunk, and they are obliged to resort to drink the next day before they can rouse their spirits sufficient to carry on their infamous trade. They are without a spark of generosity for each other and on average they die after practising their trade for two years. Not one in thirty of them reach the age of forty.

As far as I have been able judge many of them are also guilty of the crime of child murder. One fifth of those who survive their thirty fifth year, become insane, paralytic or idiotic. Most of them ascribe their crimes to seduction between the age of sixteen and twenty, and in four cases out of twenty to seduction by married men'.

In the letter the correspondent stated that he looked into the trade of some of the girls of Sheffield before they started their lives as prostitutes, and found they were made up of ordinary workers such as warehouse girls, dressmakers and servants. The unnamed doctor reflected society's disgust of such woman in the way he thought these prostitutes should be punished. He suggested that in order to rid the town of such people, he advocated that the girls are 'marched through the town in their drunken state, in order to disgust the youth of the town against such women'.

164

Unusually the letter writer didn't just show his disgust for the women, but also for the men who used their favours. He stated that 'he had always found men who associated with such women to be of tainted constitutions, often secretly addicted to drink, with feeble memory and moral purpose'. He wrote that since commencing his practice in Sheffield in 1807, he had treated 2,718 such debauched men, and he speculates that he 'doubts he could find even a hundred of them alive today'.

One unrepentant prostitute was brought before the magistrates in Sheffield in February 1840 after she had brought a charges against her husband for assault. The woman, Elizabeth Glinn appeared very smartly dressed and was able to afford the services of a defence solicitor, Mr Bramley. The magistrate expressed the view that she was very well dressed and asked her how she could afford to dress in such a manner. She told him quite openly and proudly that she was a prostitute. Mr Bramley told the court on his clients behalf, that her husband had been brought before the magistrates a few weeks previously for assault.

At that time he had been warned that he should desist from attacking his wife. The husbands solicitor Mr Broomhead then informed the court that Glinn earned her money by keeping a house of ill fame. Mr Bramley stated that Mrs Glinn had married her husband eleven years previously and she was already then in the position of being an 'unfortunate girl' and Mr Glinn was well aware of it it. He was happy to live off her earnings at that time. However the man would not stay in the town and moved from one place to another, whilst she tried to keep a home together for them both in Sheffield.

A while ago Mrs Glinn had returned back to her home and found that her husband had sold up everything in the house they had shared together, and had decamped with £70 of her money. After an absence of several months the man returned to Sheffield and demanded £10 from her. Mrs Glinn stated that she did not have it and her husband told her to demanded it from her 'bullies' [pimps]. Glinn meanwhile showed the bench a stone which she said her husband had thrown through her windows, smashing all the glass.

The husbands solicitor cross examined her at this point, but in answer to his questions, Glinn stated that she had never invited him to her house, nor had he been ill-used whilst there by any of her 'visitors'. Mr Broomhead said that her husband had told the magistrate that he wished to put all that in the past and that he wanted to start all over again. The man had said that he was prepared to reclaim her back to a respectable life and to provide for her honestly, if she would give up her profession. However the magistrate, Mr Bagshawe told him that 'she was not worth his attention'. Nevertheless he bound Mr Glinn over to keep the peace and fined him £10 and charged him another £10 as surety for his future good behaviour.

Several attempts were made by the police authorities to drive prostitution out of Sheffield. In April 1842 they launched a drive, not only to rid the town of such women, but also to attack the places where they pursued their trade. That month a man called Robert Kent, a beer house keeper was brought before the magistrates, charged with keeping a disorderly house. Constable Womack stated that at 10 am on Sunday 24 April he had gone into Kent's house and found two Sheffield girls who had several times been sent to the House of Correction for prostitution. He named them as Hannah Spencer and Ann Watkinson.

Womack told the bench that Kent had been warned many times about allowing such woman in his house, however he admitted that this was the first time that he had actually been brought before the magistrates. Kent was ordered to pay a fine of 18s, a huge amount of money at that time. At the end of the case, several gentlemen who were in the court complained of the disorderly state of an area in town called Westgate. They claiming that:

'At certain times of the day the streets were so full of disorderly persons standing out side similar disreputable houses, and as a result respectable people could not pass by without being personally insulted or by seeing things they were subject to witness.'

Immediately one of the magistrates asked where the police were when such things were happening. The Chief Constable who was present, replied that such scenes did not take place when any of his men were present. Consequently, he pointed out that the police force could not be held responsible for what happened behind their backs. He agreed that part of the town was particularly disorderly, and that the entire service of one constable would be required to keep the peace just in that one street alone.

My research into what kind of women became prostitutes in Sheffield, reveal that many of the local women were lured into the sex trade, believed initially that they were going into honest domestic service. Many of the Sheffield women who applied for such positions were persuaded that by working as prostitutes they would have a much better lifestyle. They were lured into the sex trade by being convinced that they would have plenty of money and be able to afford better clothes and be more self sufficient. In reality however they would be forced to live in brothels and have to hand over a large part of their earnings to the keeper of the house, or their pimps, leaving little for themselves.

Some women had so few belongings that they were forced to borrow clothes from the keepers of these houses, in order to go out and pick up men. None of these services were free and for which they had in the end to pay. In reality what usually happened was that most of them quickly became well known to the local police and subsequently found themselves arrested and sent to serve terms of imprisonment in Wakefield House of Correction. Only the brothel keepers and the pimps made money out of such a trade.

At the Police Commissioners meeting in Sheffield held on Wednesday 2 November 1842 a man named Mr J C Symons Esq., addressed the police authorities of Sheffield. He stated that he had visited the town some months previously in order to look into the condition of children employed in the collieries. Instead he had been appalled at the numbers of young girls acting as prostitutes in Sheffield. He too complained that the morals of the town was worse than any other place he had visited. The Police Inspector, Mr Raynor admitted that it was 'a growing evil of amazing magnitude and was sapping the morals and happiness of the community'.

The increase in prostitution in Sheffield was evident in the numbers of women brought before the magistrates. On Friday 24 February 1843 one such woman was brought before the Sheffield Intermediary Sessions. She was charged with being a common prostitute and picking the pocket of an Italian man, a visitor to the town. The man spoke little English, so his cousin appeared at the court as his interpreter. The woman, Priscilla Lee was brought in and she stated her name and said that she was aged 28 years of age, although she appeared to be much older.

She was accused by the man Benjamin Loversolli of encouraging him to buy her drinks, and getting him drunk before she robbing him. Mr Raynor was called into court and he told the magistrates that she was one of the worst characters of the town. She had been in custody for the same offence over and over again. The court decided that they could not allow her to continue ion her pestilent behaviour and ordered her to be transported to Tasmania for ten years.

By May 1844 the Sheffield Town Council were desperate to draw up by-laws to regulate such women in the town. At a meeting held at the Town Hall on Wednesday 8 May, it was agreed that;

'every common prostitute, night walker or persons loitering in the street for the purpose of prostitution, to the annoyance of householders, shall for such offence be fined 2s 6d. Second offences will lead to a fine of 5s and any subsequent fines shall be 10s. Any person found harbouring a woman trading as a prostitute and supplying her with liquor, shall be fined 10s, the second offence shall be fined 20s and any subsequent offences shall be fined 40s'.

In reality, the living conditions of some of these so called 'evil' women was one of squalour and destitution. However any research into the lives of such women, forced to earn their living in such a manner, prove it to be a squalid and dismal life indeed. Such a case was brought before the coroner on Wednesday 5 September 1845 when an inquest was held on the body of a prostitute called Ann Hepworth, aged 35 years. She was living at West Court in a wretched hovel within a few yards of the public house the Waggon, where the inquest was held. Although Ann had a husband alive, she had been earning her living as a prostitute for the last 12 years past, although for the last two years she had been very ill from an unstated disease, which was probably syphilis.

Her friends had tried to get her to visit the Sheffield Dispensary or Infirmary to be treated for this terrible disease, but she refused. Subsequently for the last few months she had been totally reliant on a younger girl called Matilda Osborne who cared for her, but also worked as a prostitute. In this manner she was able to keep them both. In order to endure the pain from her illness Ann had become addicted to alcohol and the previous Tuesday night she had once more been drunk as she and the girl Osborne went to bed. In the morning the girl found Ann dead in bed beside her.

When the police were sent to the house, they reported that the stench from the hovel was so bad that they had to obtain a quantity of chloride of lime, just to remove the smell before the house could even be entered. The inquest jury, as their first duty also visited the rooms where the body lay, were equally appalled at the conditions in which the poor deceased woman and her companion lived. The local newspaper described it as being 'a greater scene of wretchedness, misery and filth had scarcely ever been seen before'.

The conditions in which the poor woman lived were hardly better that that of her sister, a Mrs Hall who was married with children. She gave evidence as to Ann's identity, before stating that she lived in a cottage opposite the hovel where her sister lived, and which consisted of just two rooms. One room she shared with her husband and four children and the other room held her son and his wife and their two children. Mrs Hall said that she was fully aware of how her sister had earned her living, and was aware that Matilda Osborne now paid the rent and provided food from the same occupation.

The coroner who obviously had his own axe to grind, then started to grill the witness. Mrs Hall was asked if she had been aware that the woman named Osborne had been decoyed from a good place of service to the life she now led. The poor witness told the coroner that she did not know anything of Osborne until she came to live with her sister. She told the court however that she was aware that some women who lived in the area called themselves 'procurers' who had been former prostitutes themselves. These were women who were usually too old to make a living at such a position, but instead they would decoy young girls from the workhouse or places of service into prostitution.

Mrs Hall denied however that she was one of that class of women. The coroner stated that the place in which the deceased woman had lived was worse than any pigsty and there was little wonder that Sheffield was a town full of fever and disease. One of the jury pointed out that there were other parts of the neighbourhood where similar hovels were let out by women to young girls, who earned their living as prostitutes. Mrs Hall told the coroner that the owner of the property where she and her sister had lived was a man called Mr Tibbett, who she claimed was unaware of the purpose to which his property was being used.

At this point at the request of a member of the jury, a policemen was sent to bring Mr Tibbett into the inquest, but he returned to state that the man was away from home and his family did not know where he was. The jury 'in strong language' condemned the conduct of the landlord and requested the coroner to take steps to see about the matter afterwards. The girl Matilda Osborne was then called in and she stated the manner in which she earned her living. Mr Parkin, one of the Guardians of the Sheffield Workhouse, who was a member of the jury, stated that the girl had been an inmate last year and had cost the parish a large sum of money.

The workhouse authorities had found her a good place in domestic service, but without giving any notice she left her employer to rejoin her companions and make a living working on the streets. Several members of the jury entreated the girl Matilda Osbourne to leave her present course of life and apply for admission back into the workhouse and the poor witness, unable to do anything else, promised to do so.

Mr Parkin told the coroner that it was a frequent occurrence for women to be led into a life of prostitution by other women from the

West Court area of Sheffield. The only way in which such woman usually returned back to the workhouse was when they were so diseased and ill that they were driven back to enter the hospital wards for treatment. The coroner could hardly hide his disgust as the jury returned a verdict that the woman Ann Hepworth had died from an illness 'brought on by her disgusting lifestyle'.

Some of the worst brothels in Sheffield which had been described as 'nests of crime and immorality' by the Chief Constable were uncovered on 10 September 1853. The police force had been on yet another drive to try to eliminate the town of the crime of prostitution altogether. He told the magistrates that not one, but thirteen such houses had been found in the latest raid. The houses were situated in a yard off Spring Street, Sheffield. On 10 September 1853, five keepers of these houses were brought before the bench charged with keeping 'lewd and disorderly' houses.

Inspector Tasker of the Sheffield Police force asked the court to issue an order that all the houses in that particular yard be closed. He said that many of the landlords had been before the bench on several occasions for allowing drunkenness in their houses, and charged with harbouring common prostitutes. The Inspector told the magistrates that the previous Sunday morning on 4 September, he had visited all the houses owned by the five prisoners between midnight and 1 am. In every one he had found men and female prostitutes together in bed.

The Inspector added that the landlady of some of the properties let rooms out to girls as young as fifteen years of age, with no questions asked. One of the prisoners, a man named John Blyth, told the magistrate that it was common knowledge in the town as to what the houses in Spring Street were being used for. He added 'and what's more that all the houses in the yard had been brothels for over 20 years'. The magistrates told him:

'I might as well talk to the stones as to you. You are lost to all feelings of decency and morality, and nothing will make an impression on you, but to make you pay, and sending you to prison if you cannot. You are a scourge and a nuisance to society.

With so many honest ways of getting a living in these times. one cannot conceive how any person can lead the depraved life you are doing together in that yard, encouraging prostitution, drunkenness, vice and debauchery of all kinds. You are not fit to live among Christians'.

Blyth reluctantly admitted it was his second offence, so he was fined 20s by the bench and the other four keepers were fined 10s each.

The most reviled 'evil' women of Sheffield were young prostitutes who were seen as being responsible for corrupting the equally young men of the town. In February 1855 four young girls were brought before the Sheffield magistrate aged 16, 17, 18 and 19 years of age. The account that they gave to the court of how they entered the trade was all too familiar. The Chief Constable, Mr Raynor told the bench that he declined to offer any evidence against the four girls, but instead had called them as witnesses against a man called John Wilson, a lodging house keeper of Water Lane, Sheffield. His wife, Mrs Wilson also attended court to answer the charge.

The girls stated that they and other young girls were kept at the house, where they paid 1s 5d a week for lodgings, and in order to earn the rent they were encouraged to entertain young men. They told the court that they divided up the money they earned in this fashion among the other women of the house. In that manner, their 'wages of sin' paid the rent and bought them food and clothes in which to continue in their profession. Mr Rayner told the bench that some of the parents of these girls had approached him, begging him to rescue them from the hands of Mr and Mrs Wilson.

Mr Raynor claimed that he had taken the girls forcibly away from the couple and returned them back to their parents. However he said that the couple were very reluctant to be forced into giving the girls up. Mrs Wilson was also charged with pawning the frock of one of the girls she kept at the house. The magistrate told her that he was fining her husband 10s for keeping a disorderly house, and that any future charges of illegally pawning might be also brought against her at a later date.

In June 1857 the local newspaper published some crime figure which compared the statistics with those of 1848. It seems that the numbers of disorderly prostitutes had greatly increased in Sheffield during the intervening years. The report stated an incredibly low figure of just 34 known prostitutes working in Sheffield in 1845. However that figure had doubled by 1853 and it had trebled since then. The increase in number was blamed on the garrison of soldiers that had been stationed in the barracks of the town.

Three months later the magistrates were embroiled in an accusation between a prostitute and a night watchman who had given evidence against her. Mary Watson of West Lane had been accused of parading the streets for the purpose of prostitution by George Shaw Brown on his Norfolk Street beat. Watson made a counter accusation that Brown was in the habit of visiting her at the brothel on West Lane and there 'he shared in the proceeds of her infamy'. She also accused him of spending hours there with her, when he should have been on his beat.

The woman stated that she had sat up for him for many nights in order to supply him with hot coffee and 'other comforts' when he was supposed to be working as a night watchman. After passing onto her a loathsome disease from which she was still suffering, she said that he had now formed an attachment to another working girl. Since she had found out about this, she had gone to see him and asked him for an explanation. That was when he had seized her and taken her to the Town Hall where he made this charge against her. Mary denied that on that occasion she had not been on the streets for any immoral purpose and had not spoken to anyone.

Brown told the magistrates that the girl was lying and pointed out that respectable police officers who did their duty, were constantly exposed to such accusations. He admitted that he had previously been accused on a similar charge by another prostitute named Roe. He said that he knew the girl was diseased and that was the reason he had taken her into custody. Mr Raynor agreed that such accusations were regularly made against his men and that they were very difficult to prove, but he told the magistrates the girl was known to be a notorious prostitute. After listening to both side the bench sent the woman to prison for three months.

As we have seen other raids were regularly made on such houses of ill fame, but the local authority failed to drive out this abhorrent trade from Sheffield. On Wednesday 30 October 1885 yet another raid was made on such a house and several people were again brought before the magistrates. They were charged with offences under the new Criminal Law Amendment Act which had been brought out that year. The aim of the act was to suppress brothels and thereby eliminate prostitution. It was reported that plain clothes police men had been ordered to keep watch on certain of these notorious houses in order to obtain information on the men actually using these brothels.

The Chief Constable explained that despite the introduction of the new act, it was still very difficult to implement for the Sheffield Police. The first two cases that were heard by the magistrates that month underlined the difficulty. The magistrates were told that one of these notorious places on Lea Croft in Sheffield was disguised very cleverly as a shop, in order to account for men and women coming and going in and out of its doors. A man called Mr Henry Deakin occupied the shop and on Tuesday 22 October 1885, Sergeant Stone and Police Constable Buttery had been keeping an observation on the shop, when they saw, in a short space of 20 minutes, three women go inside each with a man.

Deakin who was aged 57 stated that he was a widower and lived by himself, but the bench had little sympathy for the man and informed him that under the new act, the offence was very a very serious one. The chair to the magistrates informed him that the punishment for charges under the new act had been increased threefold to what it had been previously. However because this was the first time that Deakin had appeared before the bench, they would be lenient and he was ordered to prison for just one month with hard labour.

In the next case that was heard, a man and a woman named George Stiff and Polly Goodwin were charged with keeping a disorderly house in Corporation Street, Sheffield. However, although their names were called, the defendants did not appear and warrants were issued for their arrest. It seems that just the threat of being brought before the bench and charged under the act was a deterrent in itself in some cases. Consequently the police visiting the property found that all the furniture in the house had been sold and George Stiff and Polly Goodwin had since left the town.

One of the difficulties that the Sheffield police had was in dealing with former respectable women who had been driven into prostitution by sheer need. On Tuesday 6 September 1892 a case was heard at the West Riding Court, Sheffield about a mother who had turned to prostitution to support herself and six children. Ellen Higgins had lived in Ecclesfield, and had been made a widow two years previously. She managed to find a job working in a paper mill for which she was paid 9s 6d a week. Out of this she had to pay 1s 3d rent every week, and this left her with only 8s to feed herself and the children.

Higgins told the bench that she had tried to manage for as long as she could, but when the mill closed down a few months previously, she had been forced to apply to the workhouse for relief.
There she was allowed 10s a week and allowed to live at home, but once the workhouse officials learned that she had also been acting as a prostitute, the money was immediately stopped, and she was forced to enter into the workhouse. Constable Gunstone told the court that he had known Higgins for about three years. On the 23 March he had reason to visit the house and found a man who told him he was a navvy lodging there. Since that time he had kept an eye on the house and had frequently seen her in the company of different men late at night. The magistrate ordered that the mother be sentenced to prison for 14 days. What happened to her six children whilst she served her time, we can only speculate about.

This then illustrates the lives of some of these 'evil' women of Sheffield, who turned to the oldest profession in order to make a living for themselves and their families. I would like to think that we now live in a more tolerant age and have better understanding of the problems facing working girls. But back in 19th century Sheffield, such woman had little chance of gaining anyone sympathy. Shunned by society and the legal authorities alike, they were condemned in the local newspapers, in letters to the Editor and from the pulpits of the town.

If you have enjoyed reading this book, then here are some more Sheffield books written by the same author and easily accessible to download onto a kindle device immediately or to buy in book form on Amazon.

Sheffield Books:

SHEFFIELD'S DARK TRILOGY

All proceeds from this Trilogy will go to the Sheffield Hospitals Trust (SHC) which helps support all the major hospitals in the city as a token of our appreciation for all the extremely hard work they are undertaking during this present COVID-19 crisis. Remember – All these cases are true, and many have never been written about before. They all actually happened in Victorian Sheffield.

SHEFFIELD'S DARK STREETS

This book is intended to be the first of a 'dark' trilogy about crime and murder in 19th century Sheffield. As the people of the city walk through its streets today, they are unknowingly following the path trodden by a colourful menagerie of criminals buried in its past. Like James Hill who walked hand in hand with his nephew along Moor Street, where the boys mutilated body was later found. The Wicker today is full of shops and restaurants, can you imagine that on this famous landmark, a man decided that his only way out, was to murder his wife and then kill himself?

Does your daily commute take you along Leadmill Road, it was there that James Hall murdered his wife with an axe claiming that she had been unfaithful to him. Only facing death, did the truth finally emerge. Remember that in the 19th century Sheffield had the wealth brought on by the Industrial Revolution, at a time when there was great poverty and privation. Remember that next time you are walking home, alone in the dark that Sheffield's streets saw its fair share of true crime and murder over the years, and try not to panic if one night you hear footsteps walking behind you…..

SHEFFIELD'S DARK HEART

This is the second book in the Sheffield's Dark Trilogy which reveals an underworld of determined criminals, including two young men who went to an isolated inn, fully determined to rob and kill all the inhabitants. A man who swore he would kill any bailiffs who dared to touch any of his possessions and a case of murder at the Atlas Works. There was also an abortion ring in the heart of Sheffield led by a man claiming to be a herbalist, who the police could not catch until he finally slipped up.

But also there were those lesser innocents caught up in crimes like a deaf and dumb girl, charged with infanticide, who went through the court and Assize process without understanding a word of what was said to her. A murder committed by a young woman with clear mental health problems. The book also includes stories of domestic abuse and the starvation of a wife and a child, as well as tales of women who drank too much to blot out the squalidness of their lives.

SHEFFIELD'S DARK DESIRES

The Dark Sheffield trilogy concludes with a menagerie of cases fuelled by desire and hate. For example there is a man who suffered a rejection, and in revenge plotted the death of the woman herself as well as her two sisters. Business rivalry takes a bitter twist, between two milkmen brothers, ending in something much more fatal than milk being delivered.
Hate and desire are not limited to adults... There is the case of a young boy who killed another boy he saw as a rival. Another tragic case is that of the five week old baby never wanted by it's father, and desire was truly devoid, in the case of a baby's body found in a railway carriage.

Men are not the only instigators here, there is a case of a mother killing herself and her small daughter for which no reason was ever established. There is a wife playing a double game with her lover. Within these pages, you'll find gruesome tales of areas you know or may have lived in, but a warning… these are not tales for the faint of heart!

SHEFFIELD WORKHOUSE

The records of the Sheffield Workhouse were destroyed in the bombing of Sheffield during the Second World War. However, using archive material, newspaper reports and the remaining Guardians' minutes from 1890, this book reveals the story of this feared local institution. Famously contentious, the Sheffield Board of Guardians often went against the wishes of the Local Government Board, and even of their own workhouse staff. Containing the full and fascinating histories of Sheffield's three workhouses (as well as the workhouse school and the attached farm), this book will captivate residents and visitors alike.

STRUGGLE AND SUFFRAGE IN SHEFFIELD: WOMEN'S LIVES AND THE FIGHT FOR EQUALITY

This book looks into the role of women of Sheffield and how it has evolved from the powerlessness of a woman involved in a wife sale, to the achievement of the election of its first female Lord Mayor. Using, newspapers of the period, archive material and modern photographs, this book examines how the role of women slowly changed in the city. It also highlights the militancy of the Sheffield suffragettes who not only organised demonstrations in Sheffield, but also sent groups to take part in some of the most notorious demonstrations in London. Following these demonstrations several local women were badly manhandled by police before being arrested and sent to Holloway Prison.

Adela Pankhurst tried at first to bring the women of the Sheffield WSPU to achieve the vote through peaceful means, only when the Conciliation Bill of June 1910 was dropped, did she then encourage them to take more militant action. Following the outbreak of both world wars the women of Sheffield worked in the steelworks making munitions. They worked day and night shifts often as bombs were falling about them, but when both wars ended they were abruptly dismissed, often with little notice as the men returned to take up their former jobs. Not until 2010 did the women of Sheffield get thanks or any kind of recognition for their services during both world wars. Only following a meeting with PM Gordon Brown and the erection of a bronze statue of Women of Steel in 2016, did Sheffield women truly get the acknowledgement they deserved.

SHEFFIELD BOOK OF DAYS

Taking you through the year day by day, The Sheffield Book of Days contains quirky, eccentric, amusing and important events and facts from different periods of history.
Events include matters of national importance such as the Coronation of George IV, as well as local incidents such as the Sheffield Outrages and accounts of riots in the town. There are amusing incidents from the local newspaper, for example the punishments inflicted on young boys for playing 'trip' during Divine Service and an outbreak of people being bitten by 'mad dogs'.Ideal for dipping into, this addictive little book will keep you entertained and informed. Featuring hundreds of snippets of information, it will delight residents and visitors alike.

IN THE FIRING LINE; STORY OF SHEFFIELD AT WAR 1939 - 1945

This is a unique account of the impact that the Second World War had on the city of Sheffield. Soon after the declaration of war, the government and the people of Sheffield realised that the Germans would make the city one of their prime targets, due to the importance of the steel industry. Also, for the first eighteen months of the war Sheffield had the only drop hammer in the country, which was capable of producing Rolls Royce crankshafts for Spitfire and Hurricane aircraft. Using contemporary diaries, letters, police accounts and other archive material, this book reveals how, despite heavy bombing, the people of Sheffield refused to be intimidated.

It looks at the events that were happening in the city during the countdown to the war, such as the evacuation of the children not only to other safer districts, but to the Dominions, and the development of the Sheffield Home Guard, who started out as 'Dads

Army' but were sent to London to relieve its Home Guard when the capital was under heavy fire from German rockets. Also included is a description of the protection of the dams above Sheffield and how the Ladybower reservoir was used as a training ground for the 'Dambusters'.Finally, there are accounts not only of Sheffield men who were taken as prisoners of war, but how the police dealt with the German and Italian prisoners at Lodge Moor Camp.

SHEFFIELD CRIMES

This volume collects together the most shocking criminal cases from Sheffield Victorian newspapers. These grisly cases will transport the horrified reader back to a time when horse drawn carriages clattered through the streets of the city, and the towns gin palaces and music halls teemed with thieves, drunkards and fallen women. In the age where the gap between rich and poor was enormous, crime was understandably rife - and the penalties for it dreadful. Filled with infamous historical cases – including grave robbing, murder, poisonings, infanticide , bigamy and daring jewel and garrotte robberies – and richly illustrated with photographs from private collections and from local archives *Sheffield Crimes* will fascinate residents, visitors and historians alike.

MURDER AND CRIME IN SHEFFIELD

The grim and bloody events in this book, many of which have not been written about for more than a century, reveal the dark heart of Victorian Yorkshire. These crimes reflect the poverty and squalor in which many of Sheffield working class lived. Some of these gruesome tales would not look out of place in a work of fiction, a body abandoned in the middle of the street, a man murdered by his wife and her lover and a daring case of highway robbery. Most took place in notorious areas of Sheffield where domestic violence and crime were rife – where some neighbourhoods ignored the shouts and screams of the unfortunate victims because they were so used to hearing them. Richly illustrated with archive and modern photographs, this gruesome collection will fascinate anyone with an interest in Sheffield's dark past

Printed in Great Britain
by Amazon

69061577R00108